Creative Keyboard Presents
Great Literature for Piano

Baroque – Classical – Romantic

BOOK VII
ADVANCED SONATAS

Researched and Compiled by
GAIL SMITH

EVANSTON PUBLIC LIBRARY
1703 ORRINGTON AVENUE
EVANSTON, ILLINOIS 60201

© 1996 BY MEL BAY PUBLICATIONS, INC., PACIFIC, MO 63069.
ALL RIGHTS RESERVED. INTERNATIONAL COPYRIGHT SECURED. B.M.I. MADE AND PRINTED IN U.S.A.

Visit us on the Web at http://www.melbay.com — E-mail us at email@melbay.com

Foreword

In early 19th-century Germany, the purchase of a piano commanded the interest of the new owner's entire community. The German family that ordered the piano first made a down-payment in cash. Upon completion of the piano, they paid for the balance in corn, wheat, potatoes, poultry, and firewood.

On the day that the piano was to be delivered to the new owner, the town held a festival. A band of musicians headed the procession, followed by the proud piano maker, who was borne on the shoulders of his assistants. Flowers and wreaths decorated the horse-drawn wagon which held the precious piano. Musicians, schoolmasters, and dignitaries marched in the rear.

At last the piano arrived at its destination. The delighted new owners greeted the procession warmly. The local clergyman said a prayer, blessing the new instrument as well as its craftsmen. The mayor delivered an address; the schoolmaster, doctor, and other dignitaries gave speeches. Finally, the men's chorus sang. When the piano was properly installed in its new home, everyone enjoyed a banquet and danced in celebration of this happy occasion.

In contrast, today the purchase of a piano seems no longer to be a cause for festivity and joy. Unfortunately, our generation takes such purchases for granted. We have forgotten what a treasure and gift a piano can be. We have also forgotten what a treasure and gift the great composers have given us through their beautiful musical compositions for the piano.

This new piano literature series rediscovers the "rare jewels" of piano literature. After years of research and meticulous assessment of the composers of Baroque, Classical, and Romantic music, this exciting "quest for the best" has led to a new series of eight graded books . . . all containing original compositions by the masters.

The series begins with the most easily mastered compositions, progressing to the more advanced and musically difficult selections. Pianists on all levels will enjoy this challenging, thorough, and diversified collection of piano music. In addition, an interesting biographical sketch of each composer will make these selections more meaningful to the student.

Just as flowers and wreaths decorated the horse-drawn wagon that delivered the new piano to the fortunate German villager, likewise flowers and wreaths decorate each book in this series. They serve as a reminder for us all to treasure each selection we learn and to be thankful for our magnificent musical heritage.

Gail Smith

Contents
Book Seven

Sonata Prima .... Johann Kuhnau 5
   (The Battle of David and Goliath)

Sonata in B-flat (Op. 47, No. 2) .... Muzio Clementi 24

Sonata in D (K. 576, composed in 1789 .. Wolfgang Amadeus Mozart 49

Sonata in G Minor (Op. 105) .... Felix Mendelssohn 74

Sonata in E Minor .... Joseph Haydn 99

Sonata Pathetique (Op. 13) .... Ludwig Van Beethoven 118

Johann Kuhnau
(April 2, 1660 - June 5, 1722)

Kuhnau was a notable German clavier composer. After being a choirboy, Johann's first job was as cantor at Zittau. He moved to Leipzig, where in 1684 he became organist at St. Thomas's. Four years later Kuhnau founded a concert series there and became musical director of the University. Meanwhile, he also found time to qualify as an advocate at law and also to make translations from Hebrew, Greek, Latin, Italian, and French. He even wrote poetry. Kuhnau is credited with being the very first composer to write sonatas in several movements which were not merely suites or dance tunes. He wrote two sets of sonatas; the second set was based on Bible stories. The sonata in this volume tells the famous story of David and Goliath.

Sonata Prima
(The Battle of David and Goliath)
Il Combattimento trà David e Goliath.

Johann Kuhnau
(1700)

Le bravate di goliath. (Goliath's stamping and ranting)

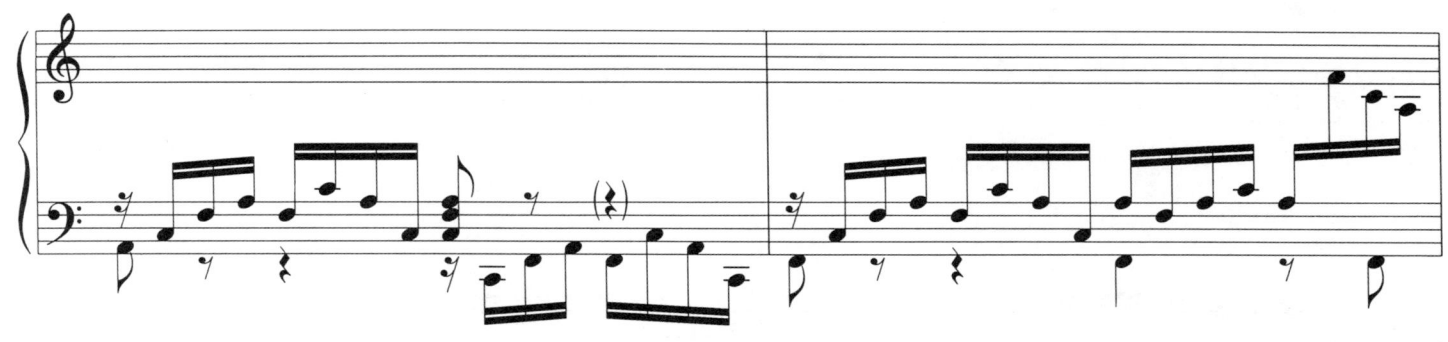

Il tremore degl'Israliti alla comparsa del Gigante, e la loro preghiera fatta a Dio.
(The trembling of the Israelites, and their prayer to God at the sight of this horrid enemy)

Il Coraggio di David, ed il di lui ardore di rintuzzar l'orgoglio del nemico spaventevole, colla sua confidenza messa nell'ajuto di Dio.
(The steadfastness at Uavia, his urge to crush the Giant's boastful defiance, and his childlike trust in God's help.)

Il combattere frà l'uno e l'altro e la loro contesa.
(The challenging words exchanged between David and Goliath, and the fight itself.

Vien tirata la selce colla frombola nella fronte del Gigante.
(The stone is slung into Goliath's forehead)

casca Goliath. (Goliah is killed.)

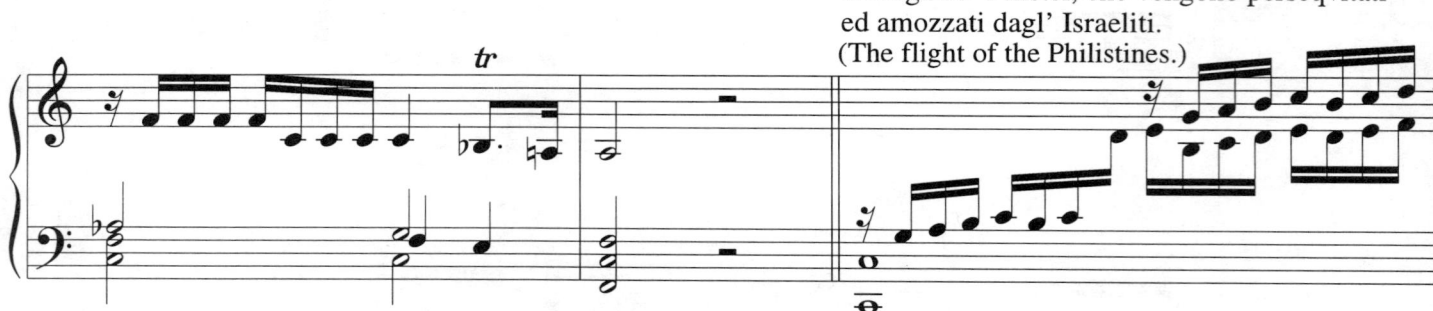

La fuga de' Filistei, che vengono perseqvitati ed amozzati dagl' Israeliti.
(The flight of the Philistines.)

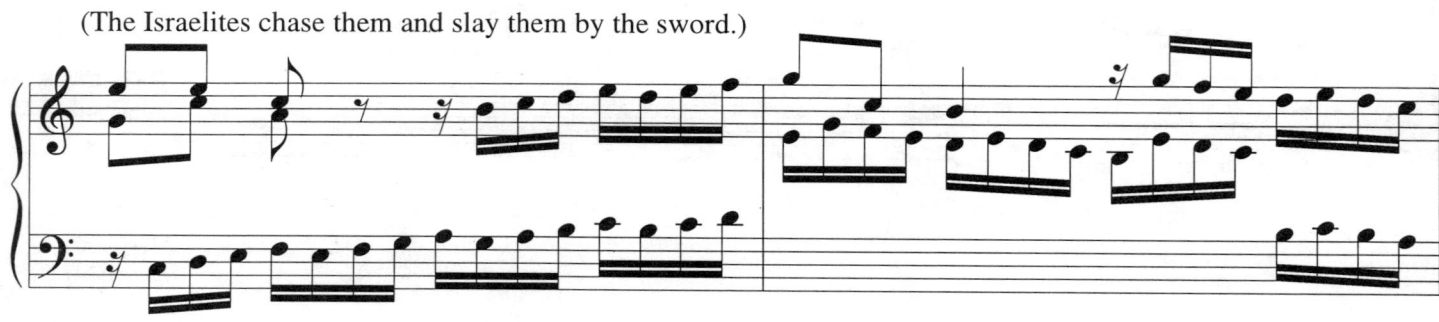

(The Israelites chase them and slay them by the sword.)

La gioia degl' Israeliti per la loro Vittoria.
(The rejoicing of the Israelites at this victory.)

Il Concerto Musico delle Donne in honor di Davide.
(The Concert to the glory of David, performed by the women in choirs.)

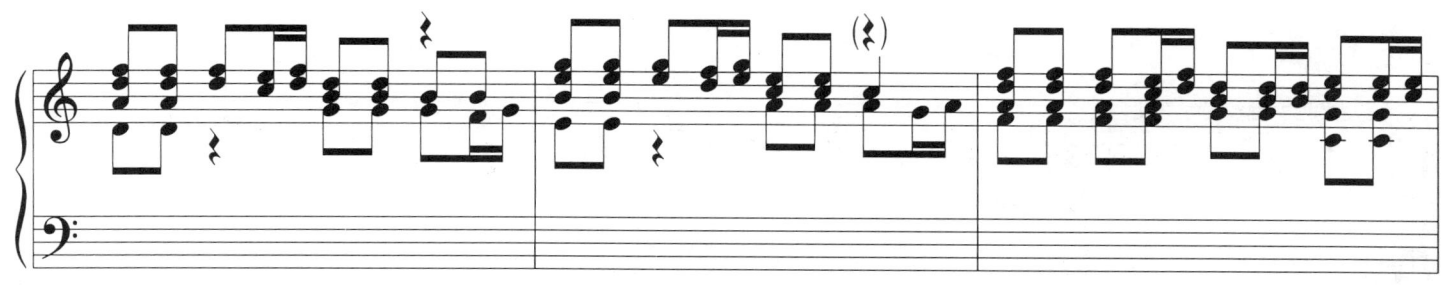

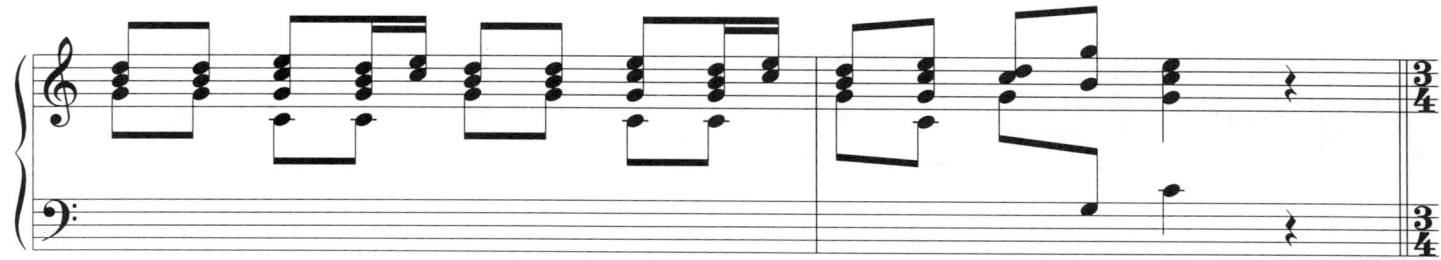

Il Giubilo comune, ed i balli d'allegrezza del Populo.
(And finally the general happiness which shows itself in an abundance of dancing and frolicking.)

Muzio Clementi
(1752-1832)

When Muzio Clementi was fourteen years old he went to England, where he lived the rest of his life. He became interested in the making of pianos and was associated with the firm Clementi and Company (later Collard and Collard); it is said that he gave the Broadwoods much advice in the making of their "grand" piano.

Clementi also was a founder of piano technique and published a work called *Gradus ad Parnassum*. These piano studies were needed to develop a technique for the new instruments.

Clementi made his mark not only as a composer, pianist, and publisher, but also as a teacher. His most famous students included Johann Baptiste Cramer, Ladislaus Dussek, Johann Nepomuk Hummel, Ignaz Moscheles, and John Field.

During his lifetime, Clementi composed over a hundred piano sonatas. The sonata included in this book is one of his very best; in fact, he played it at a historic contest with Mozart in 1781. No verdict was reached, however. It is interesting to note that Mozart later used the theme from Clementi's sonata in his overture to *The Magic Flute*.

Sonata in B-flat
(Op. 47, No. 2)

Muzio Clementi

Allegro con brio

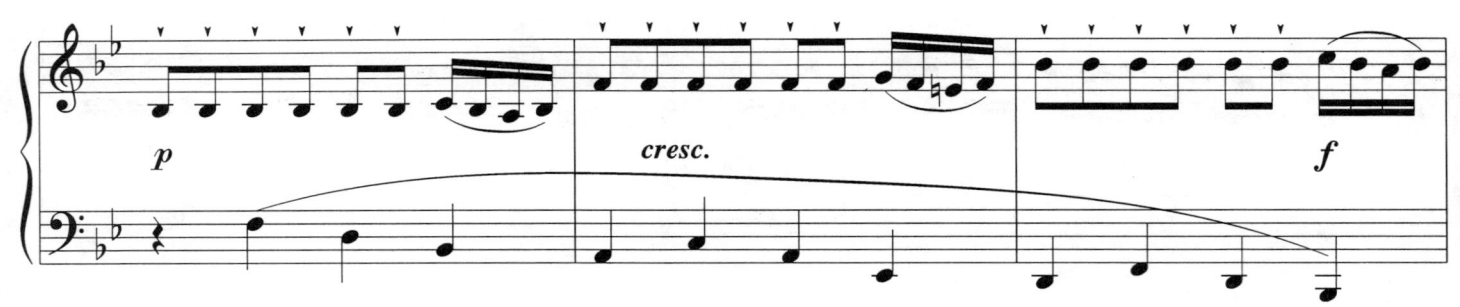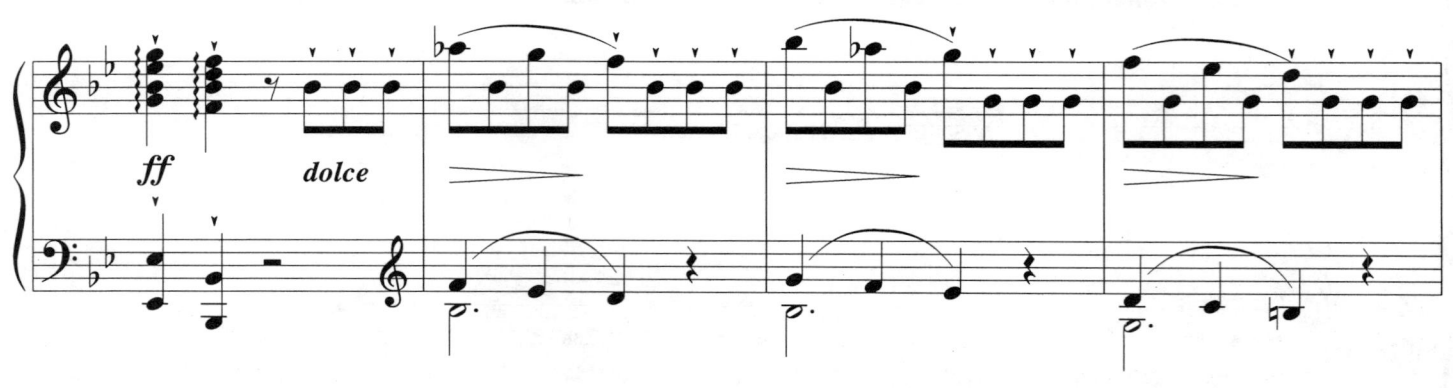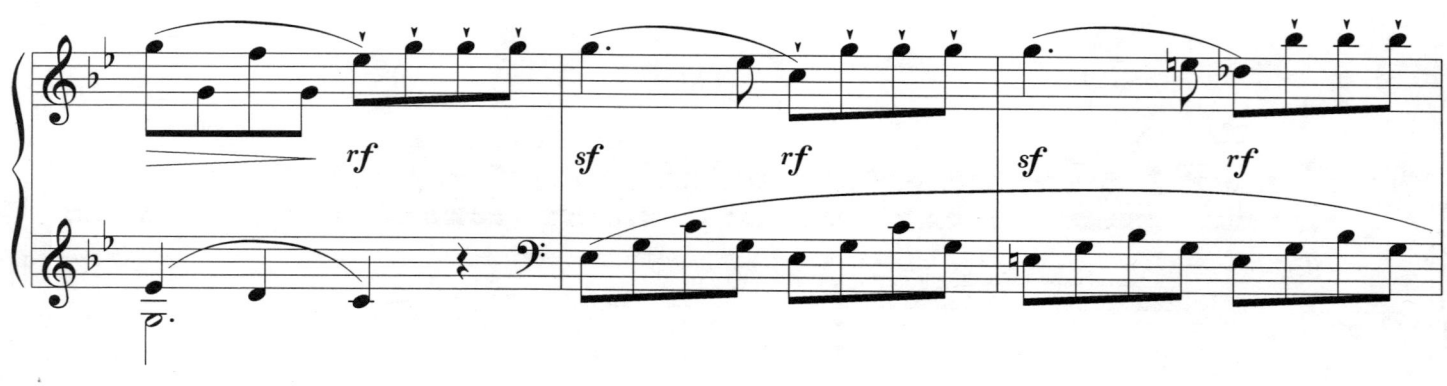

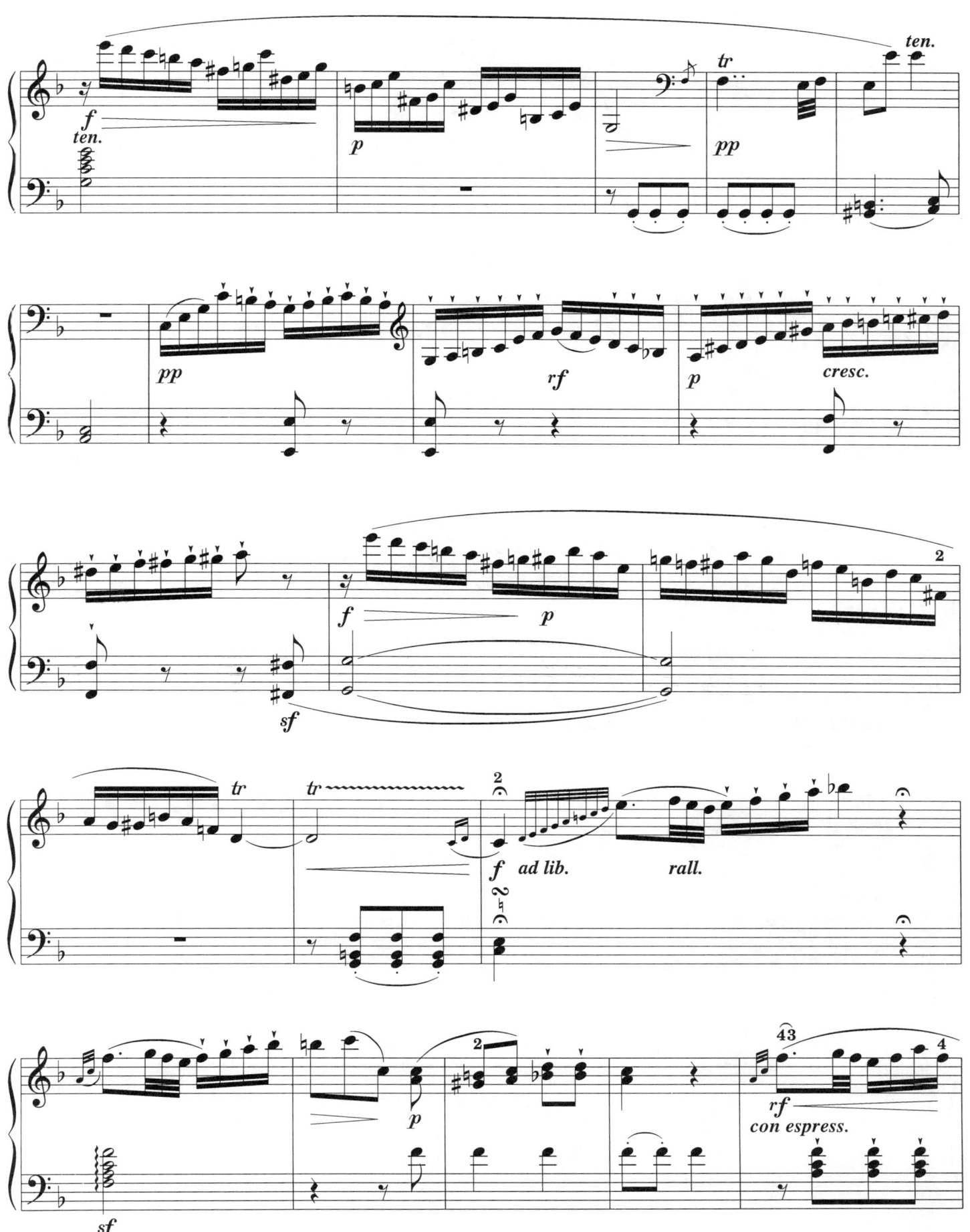

37

Rondo Allegro assai

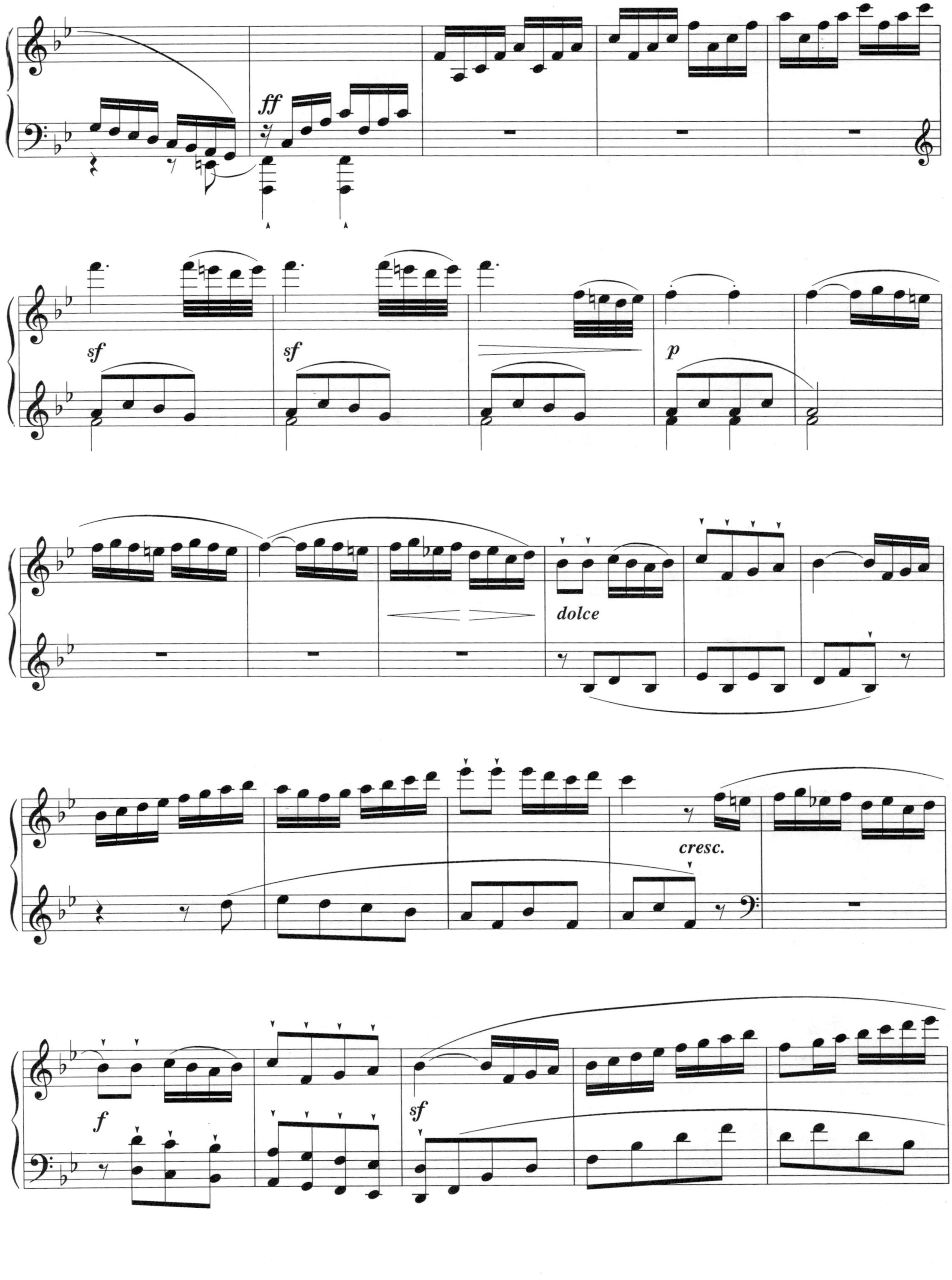
ff
sf
sf
p
dolce
cresc.
f
sf

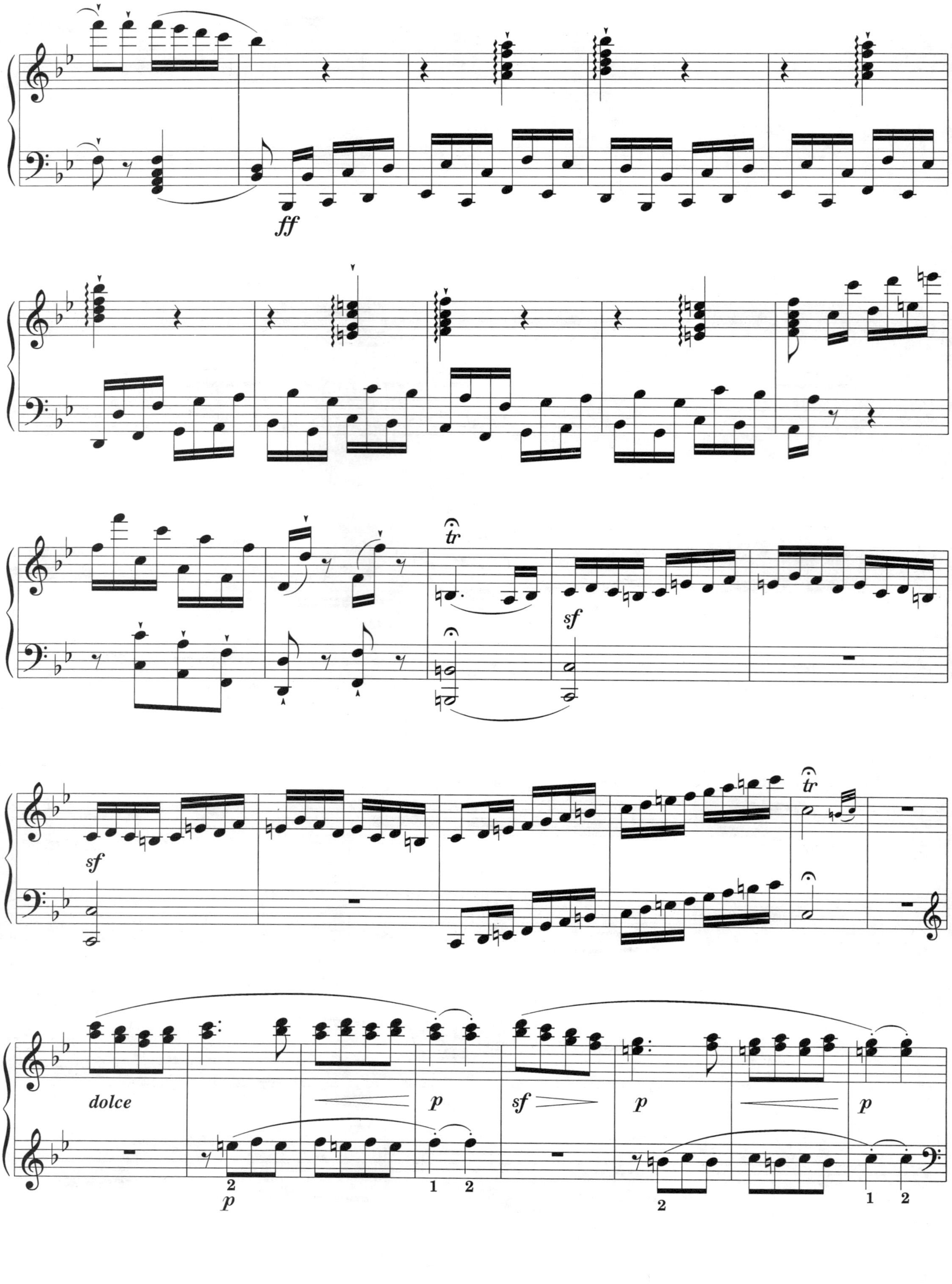
ff
tr
sf
sf
tr
dolce
p
p
sf
p
p
2
1 2
2
1 2

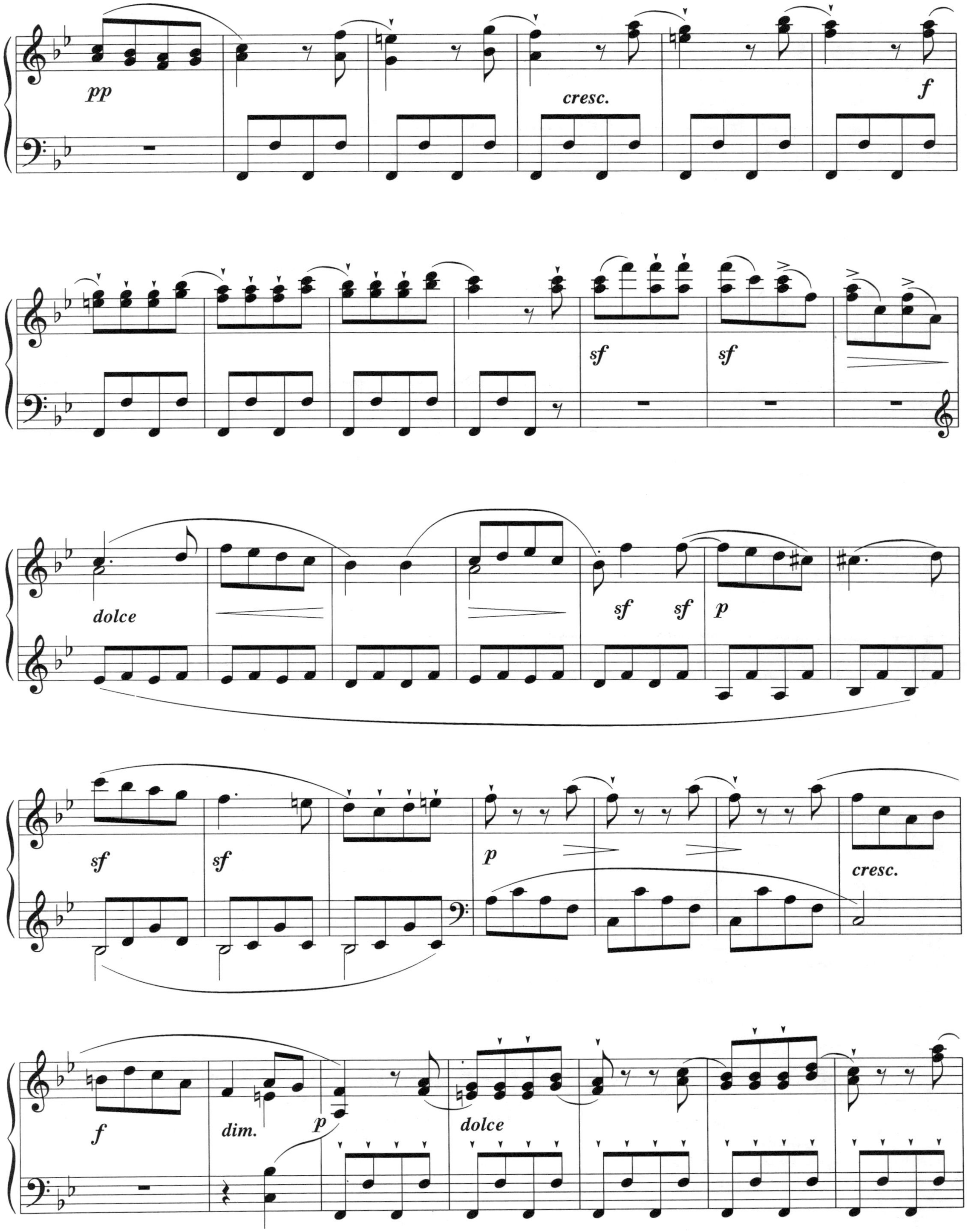
pp
cresc.
f
sf
sf
dolce
sf
sf
p
sf
sf
p
cresc.
f
dim.
p
dolce

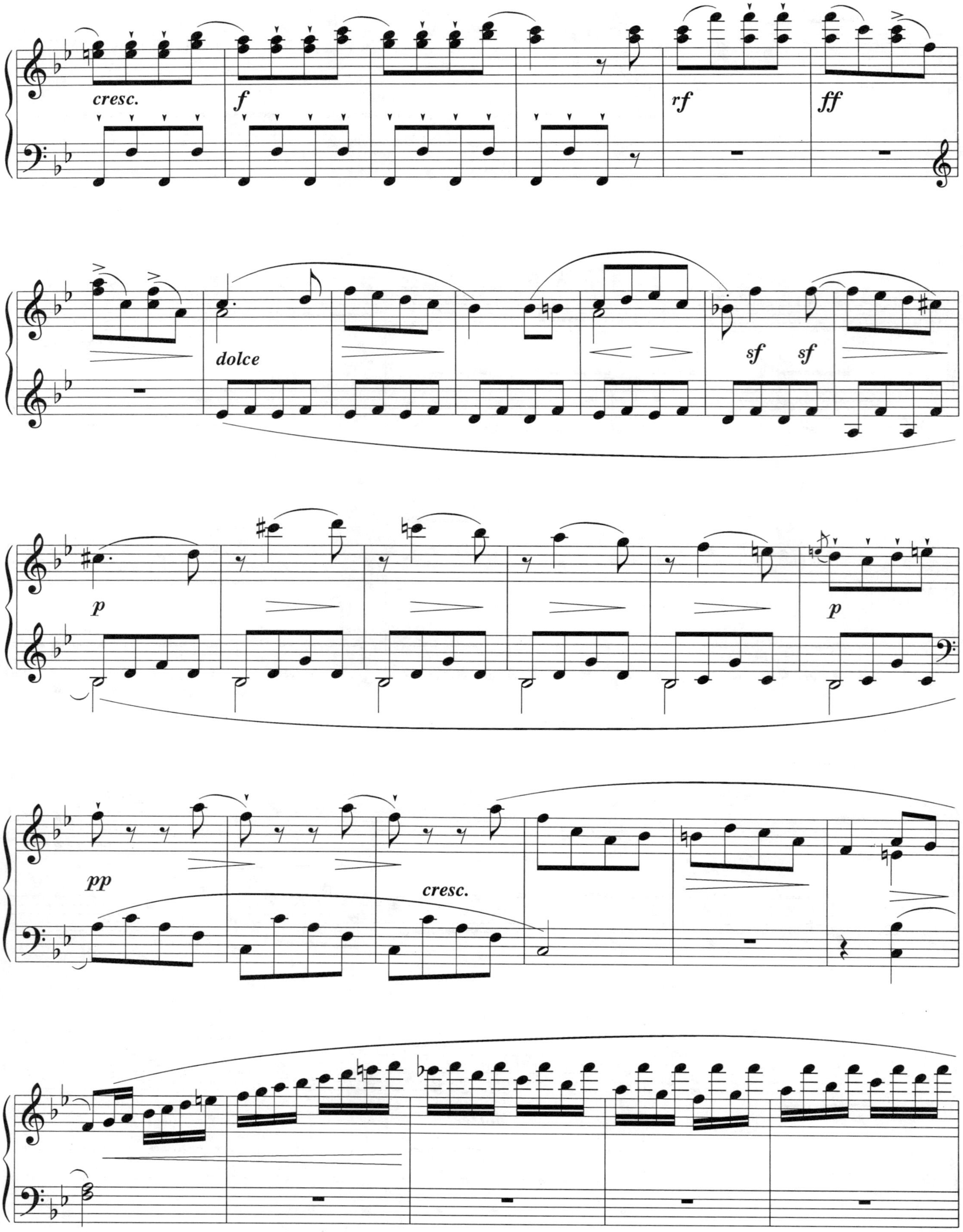
cresc.
f
rf
ff
dolce
sf
sf
p
p
pp
cresc.

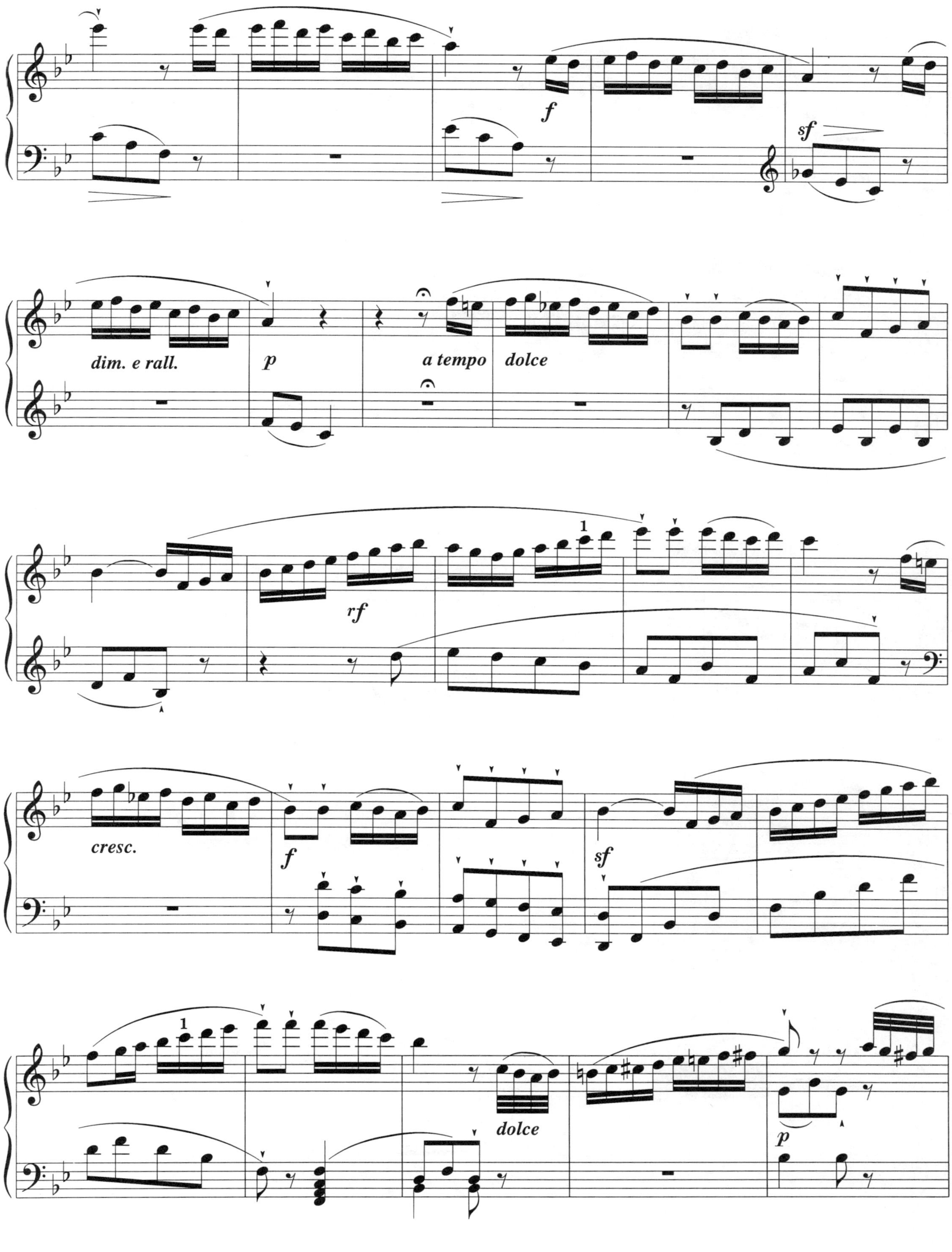
f
sf
dim. e rall.
p
a tempo
dolce
rf
cresc.
f
sf
dolce
p

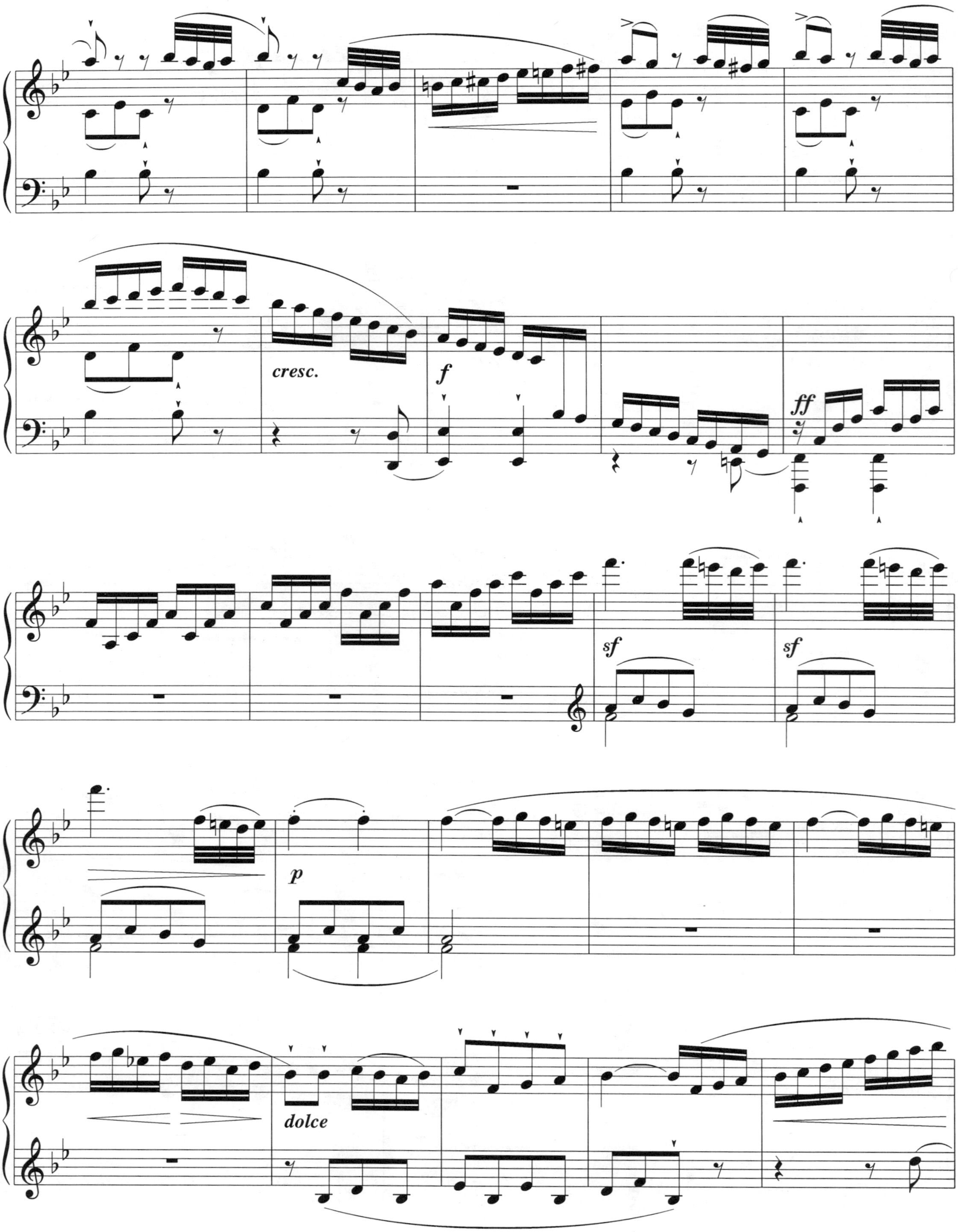
cresc.
f
ff
sf
sf
p
dolce

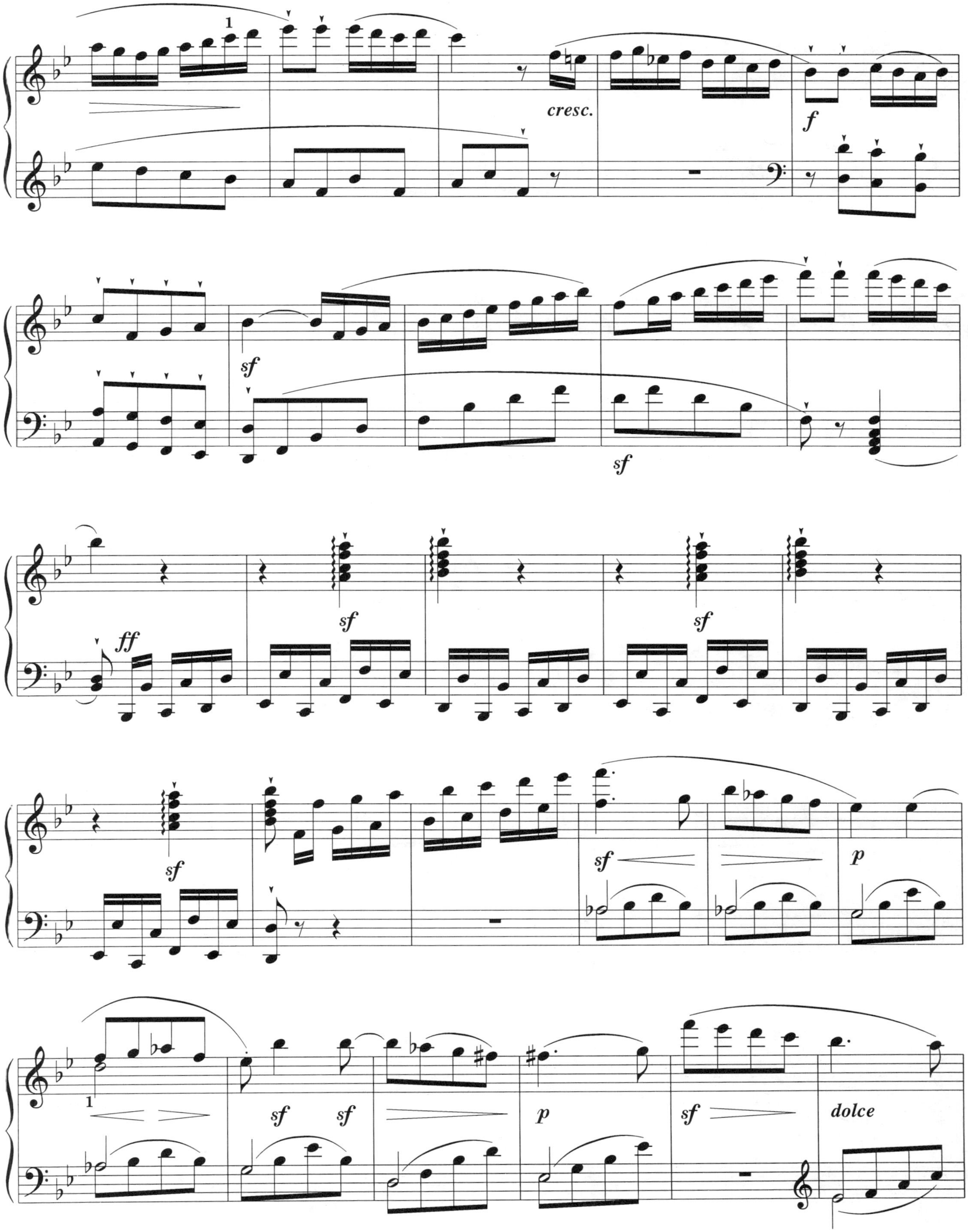
1
cresc.
f
sf
sf
ff
sf
sf
sf
sf
p
1
sf
sf
p
sf
dolce

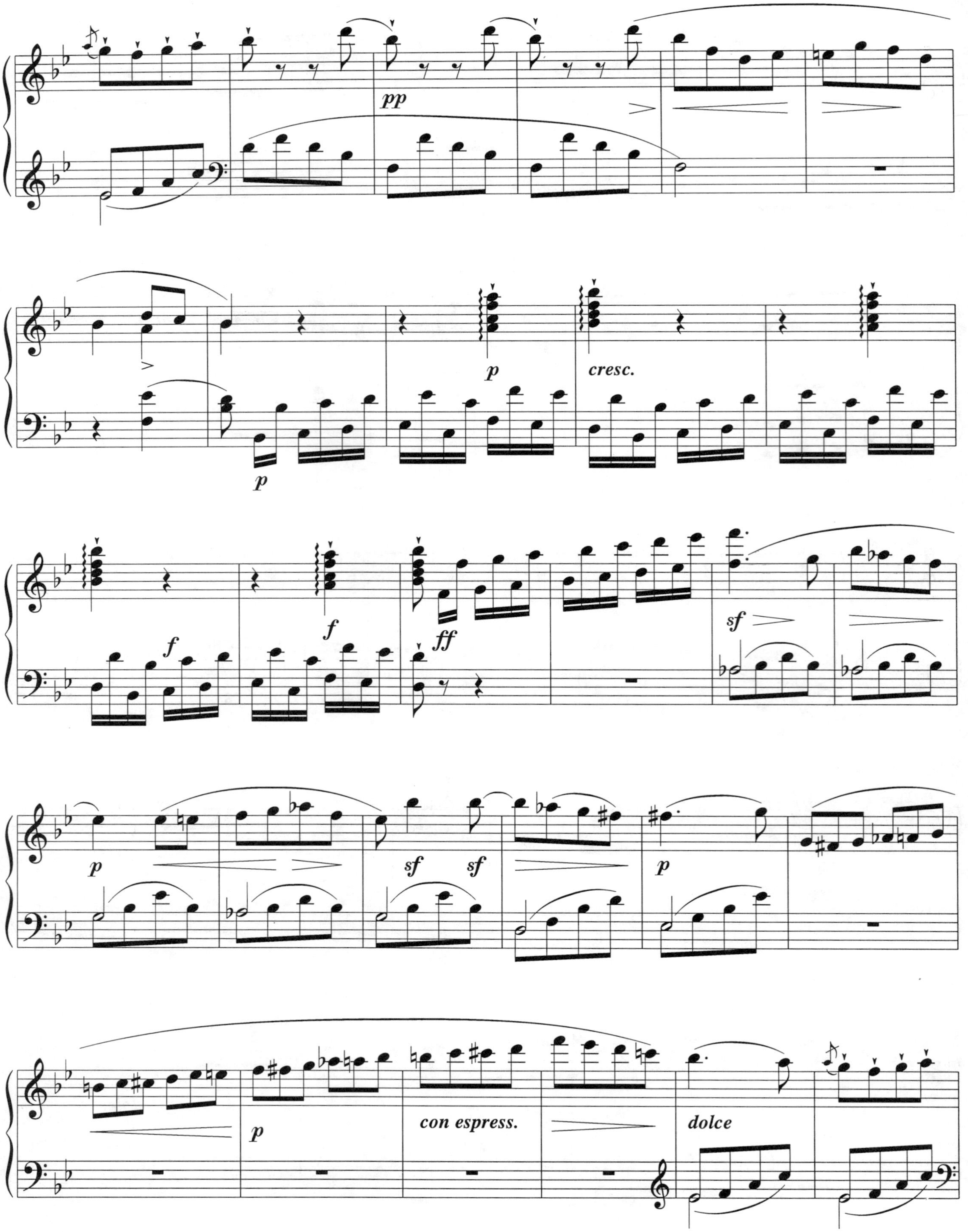
pp
p
p
cresc.
f
f
ff
sf
p
sf
sf
p
p
con espress.
dolce

47

Wolfgang Amadeus Mozart
(January 27, 1756 – December 5, 1791)

Mozart and his older sister showed amazing musical talent at a very young age. Their father, Leopold, decided to commercialize their gifts and set up concert tours in many cities, including Munich, Vienna, Paris, and London. The concerts were very successful, and the children often played for royalty. Mozart began composing at age 5 and continued writing beautiful music all his life.

Sonata in D
(K. 576, composed in 1789)

Wolfgang Amadeus Mozart

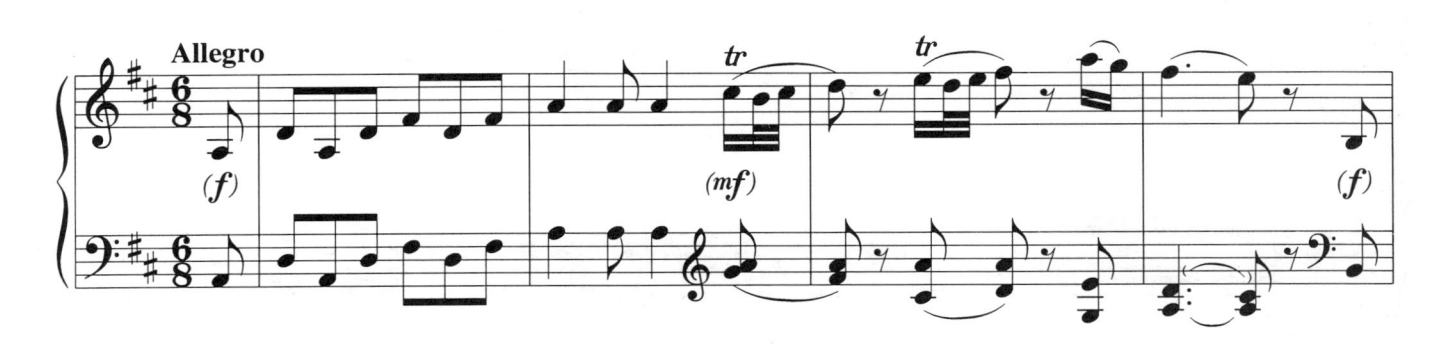

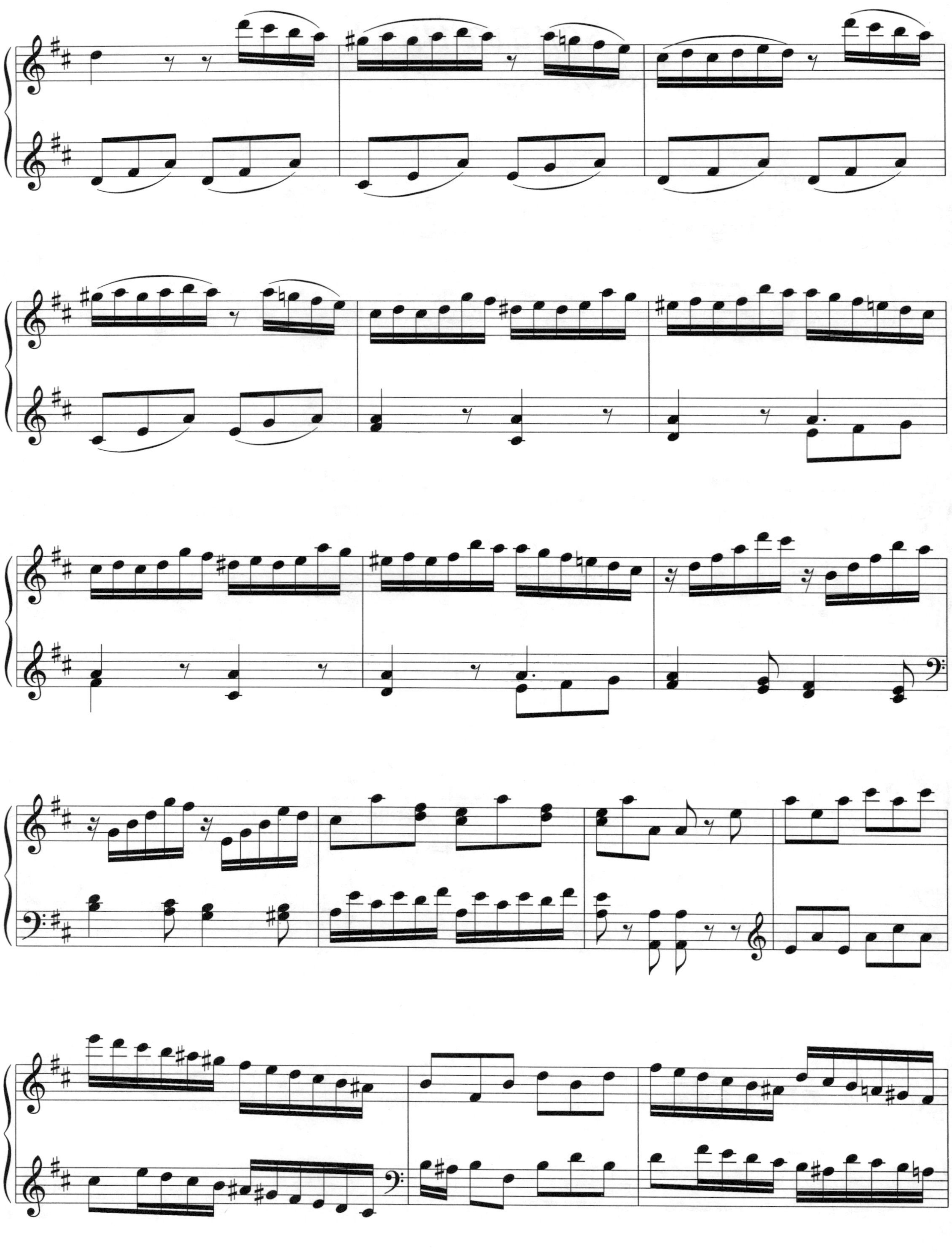

51

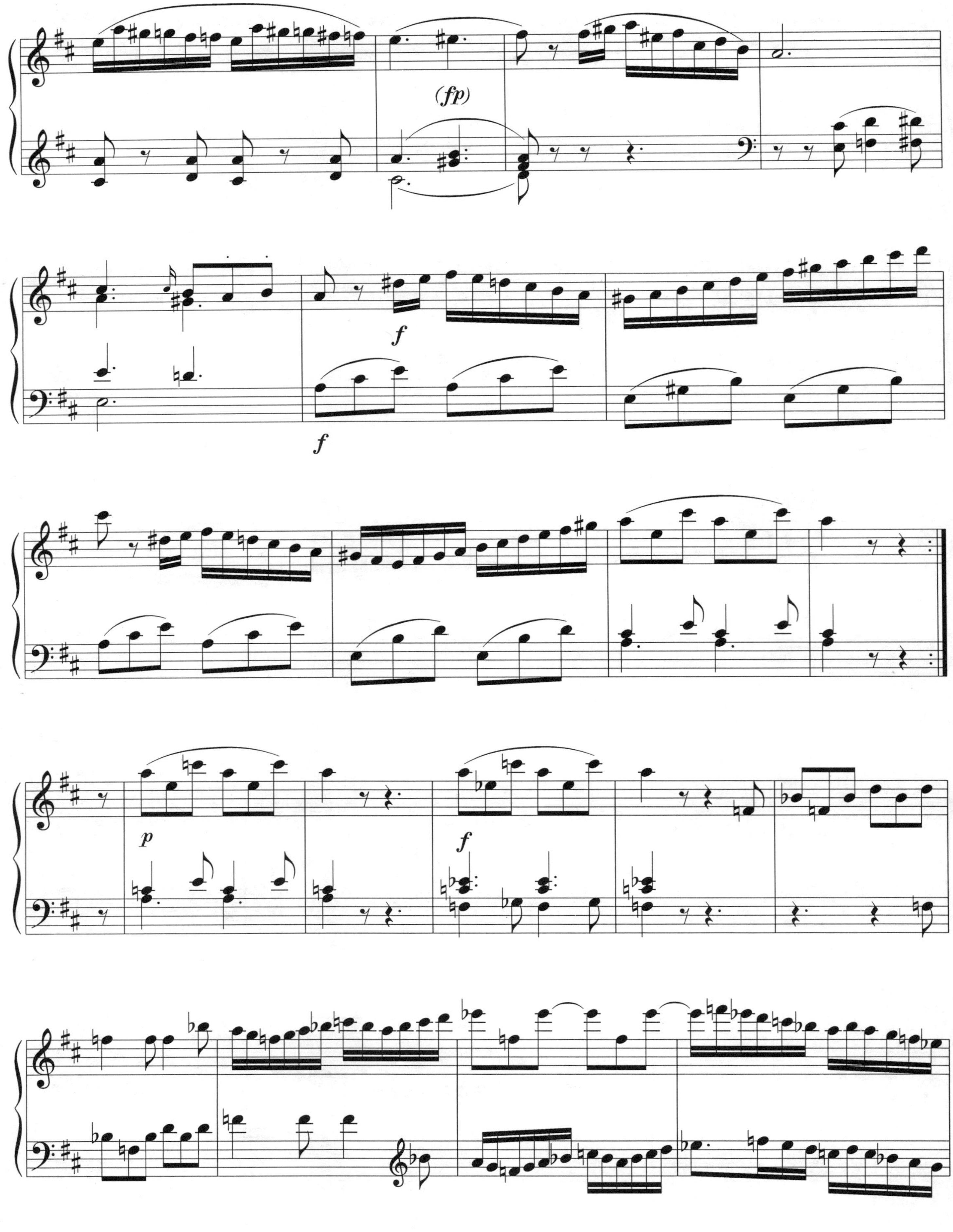
(fp)
f
f
p
f

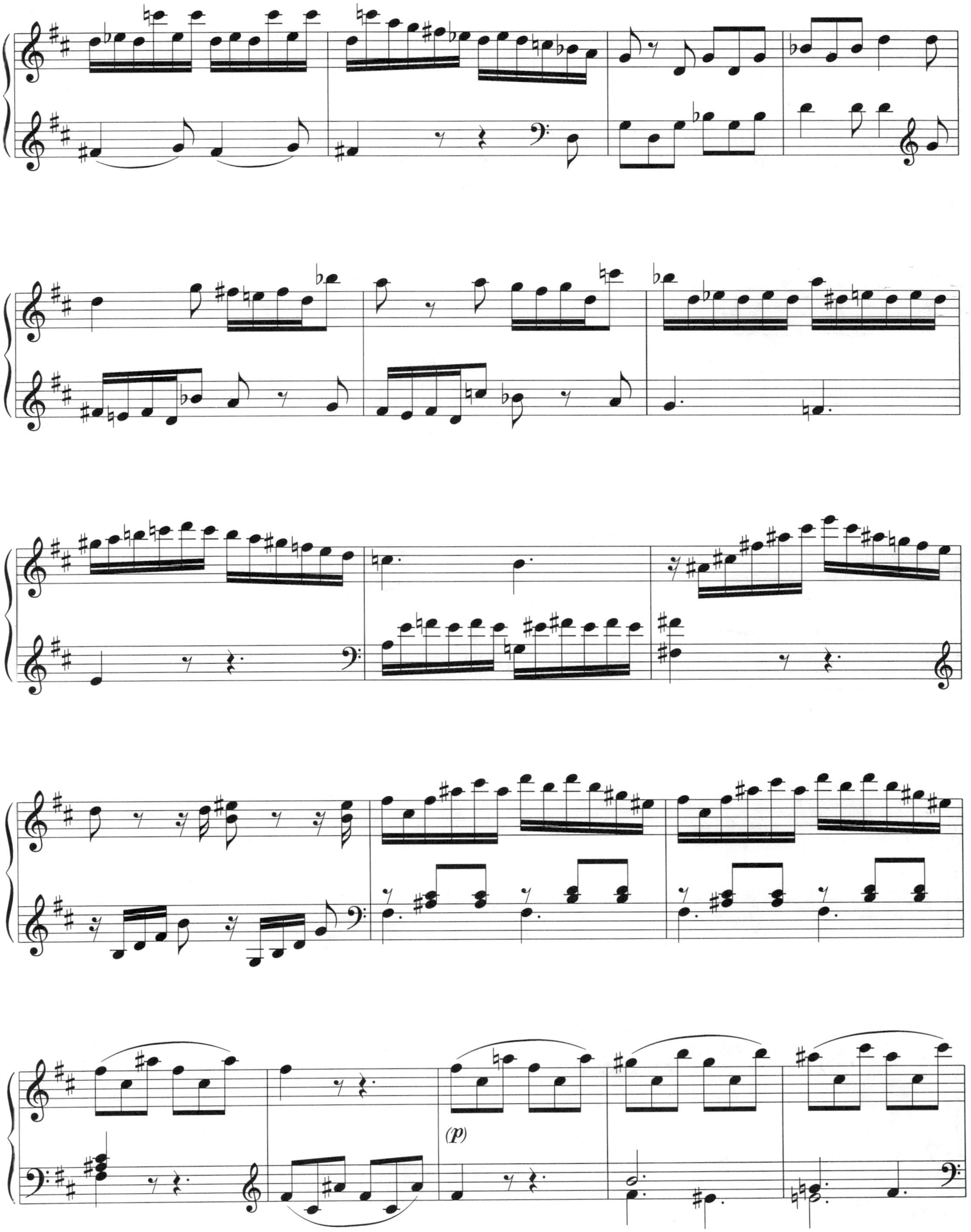
(p)

* The A's in the left hand are again lacking in the Vienna source.

54

55

56

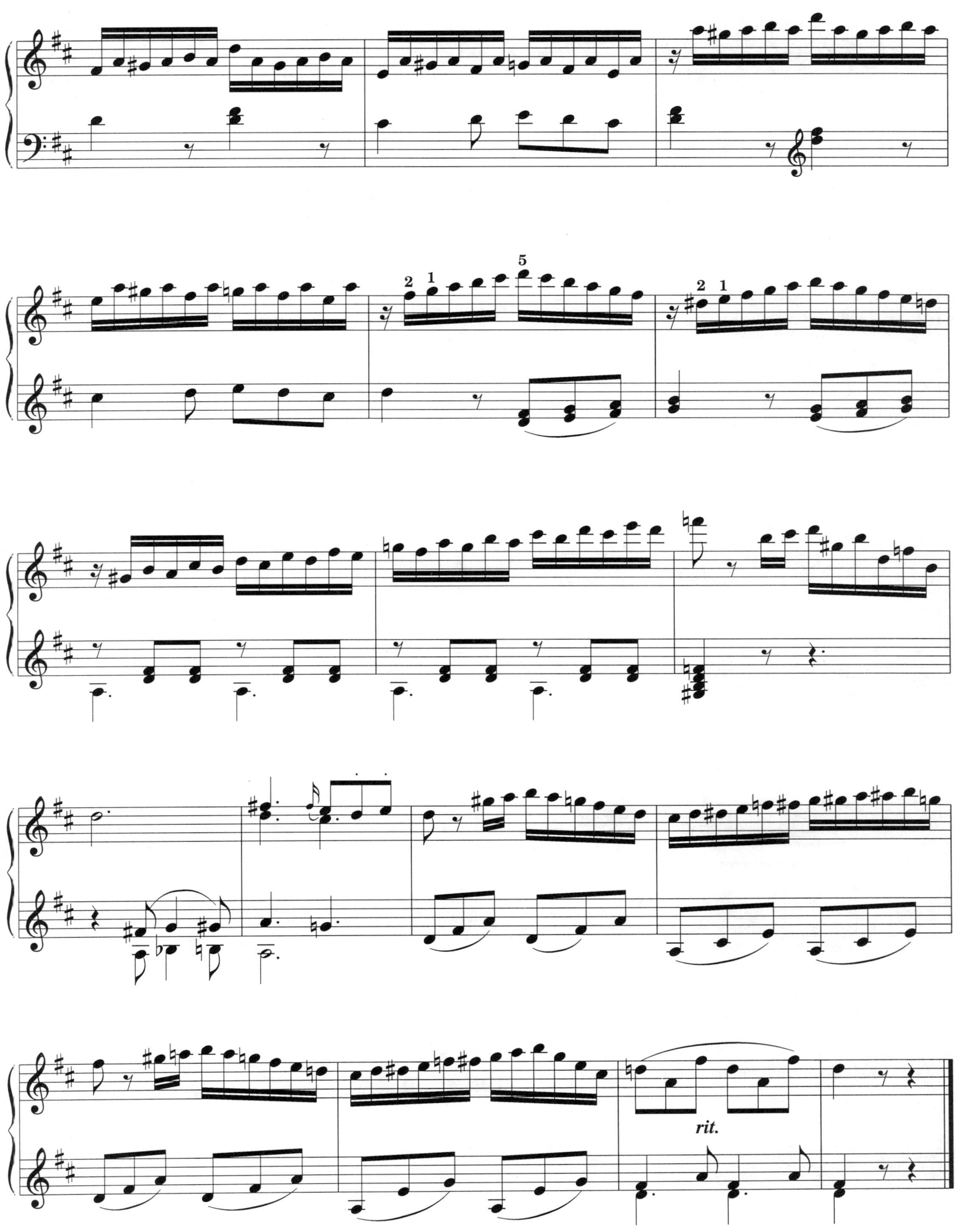
2 1
5
2 1
rit.

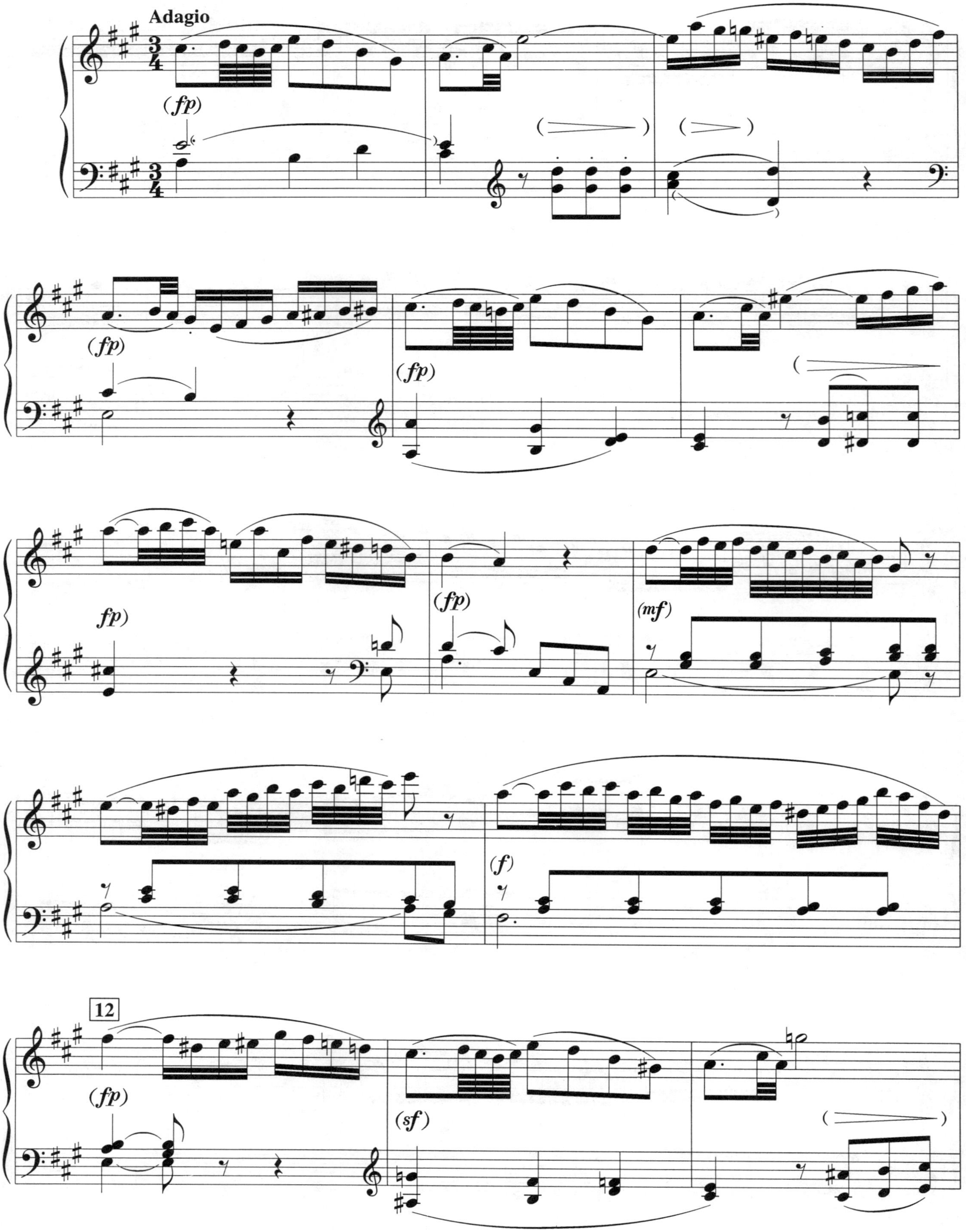
Adagio
(fp)
(fp)
(fp)
fp)
(fp)
(mf)
(f)
12
(fp)
(sf)

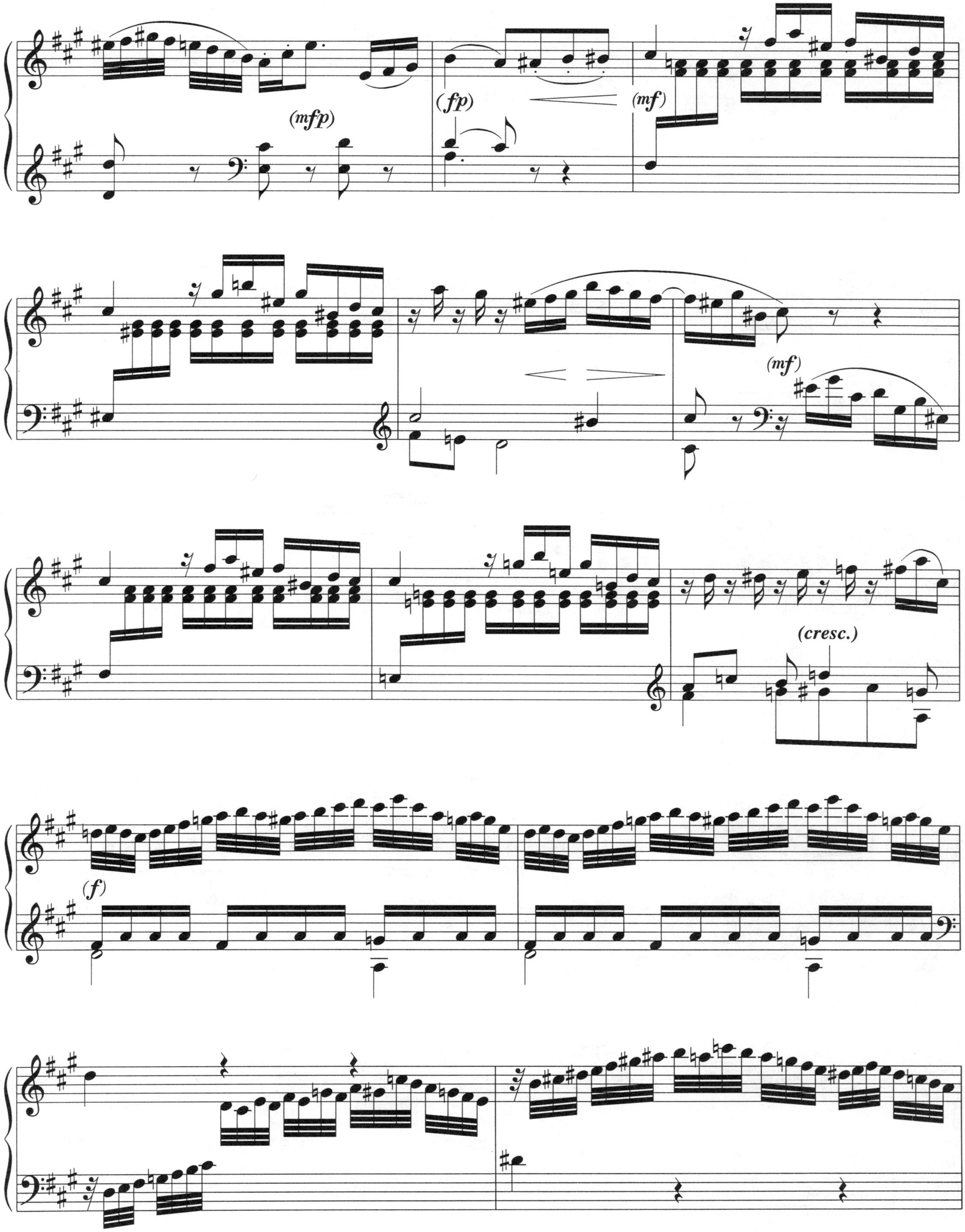
(mfp)
(fp)
(mf)
(mf)
(cresc.)
(f)

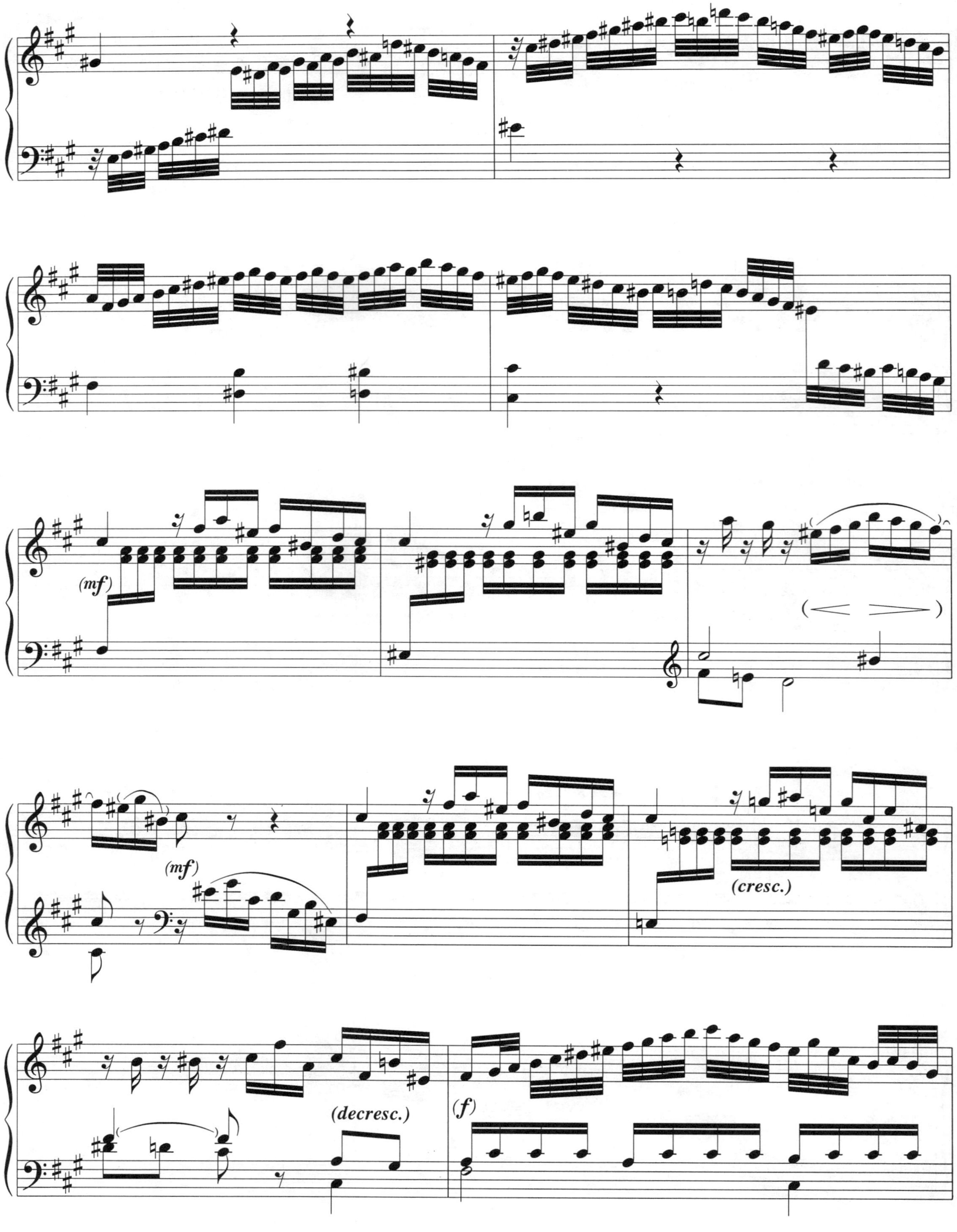

(mf)
(mf)
(cresc.)
(decresc.)
(f)

61

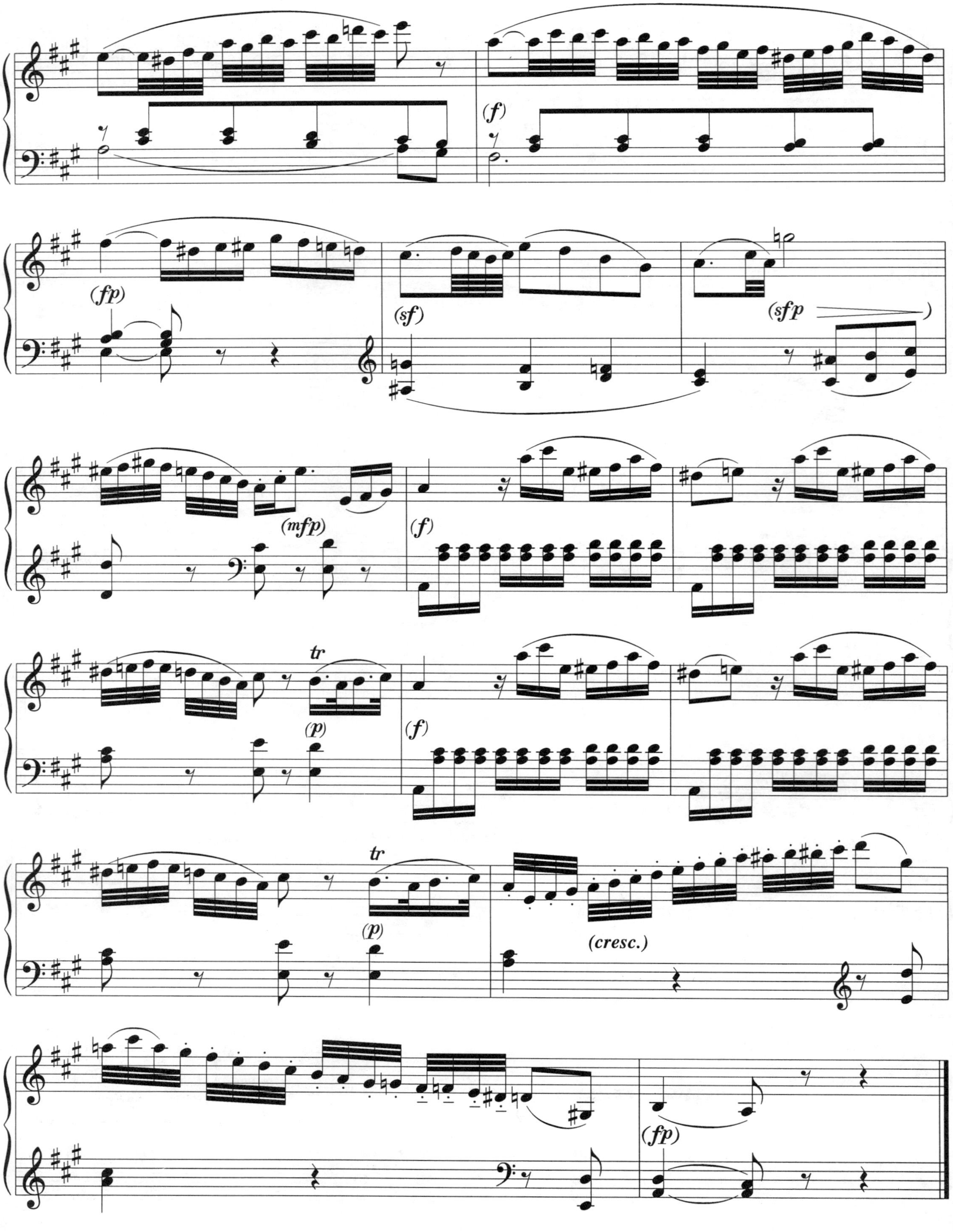
(f)
(fp)
(sf)
(sfp
)
(mfp)
(f)
tr
(p)
(f)
tr
(p)
(cresc.)
(fp)

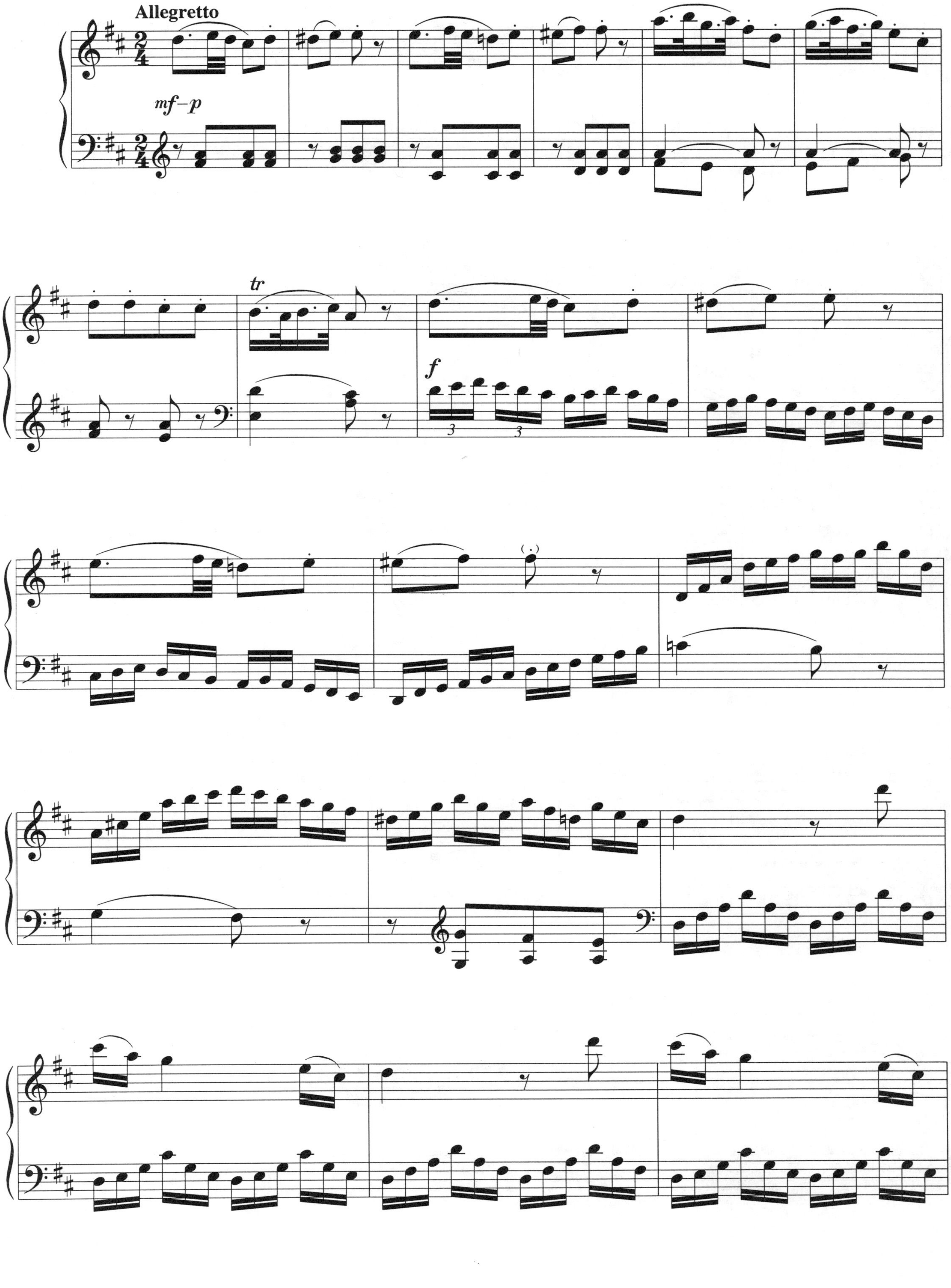
Allegretto
mf–p
tr
f

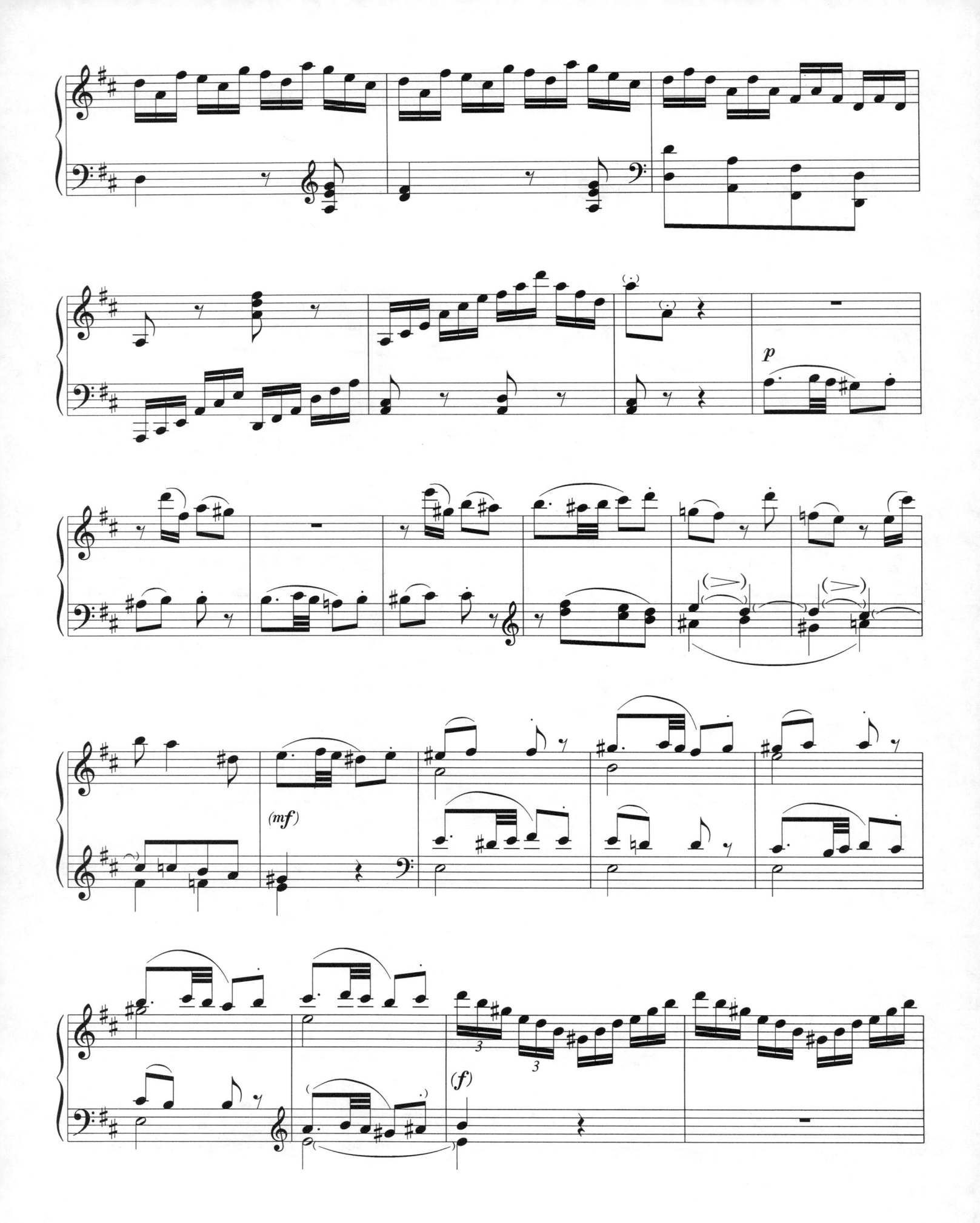
p
(mf)
(f)

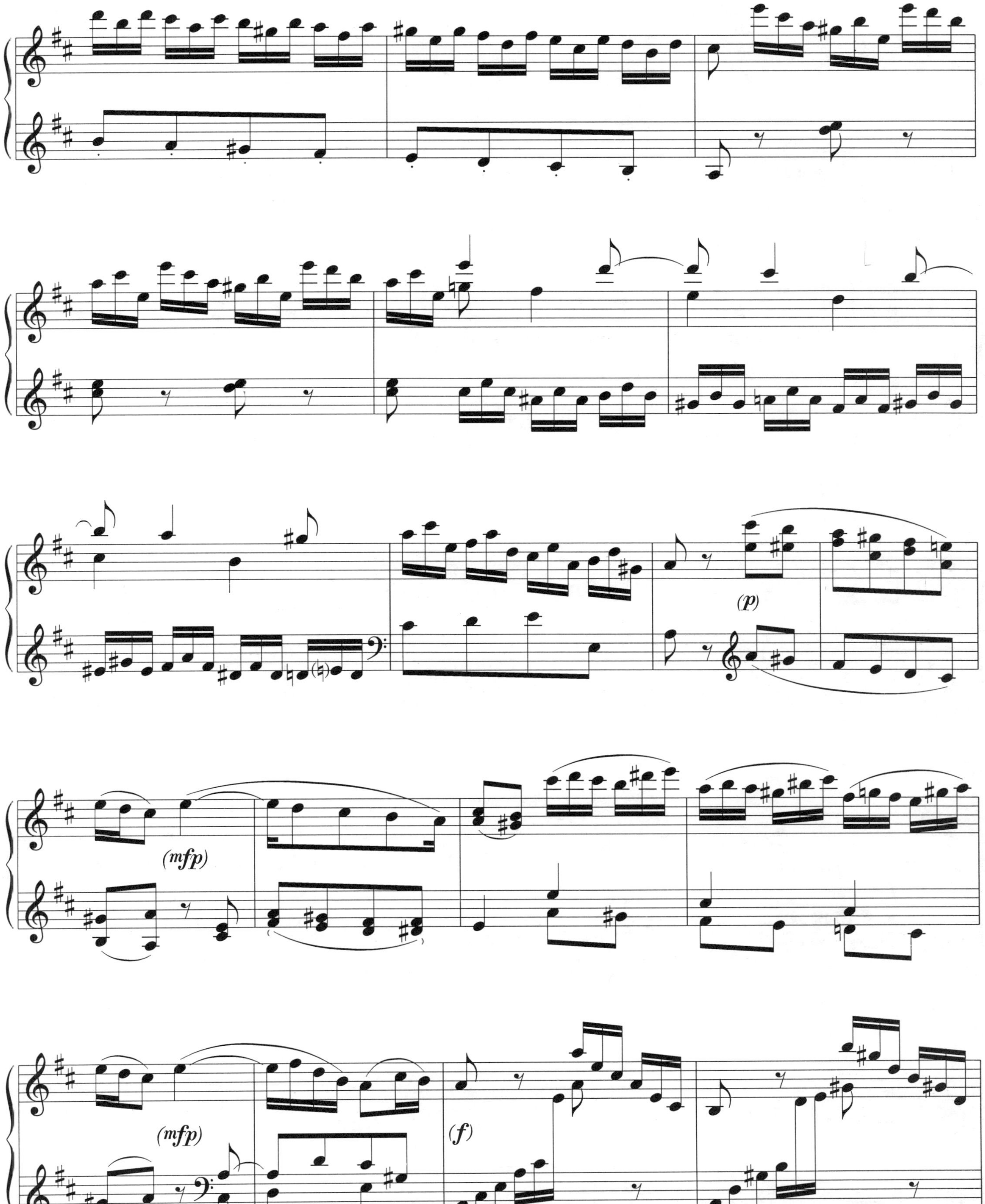
(p)
(mfp)
(mfp)
(f)

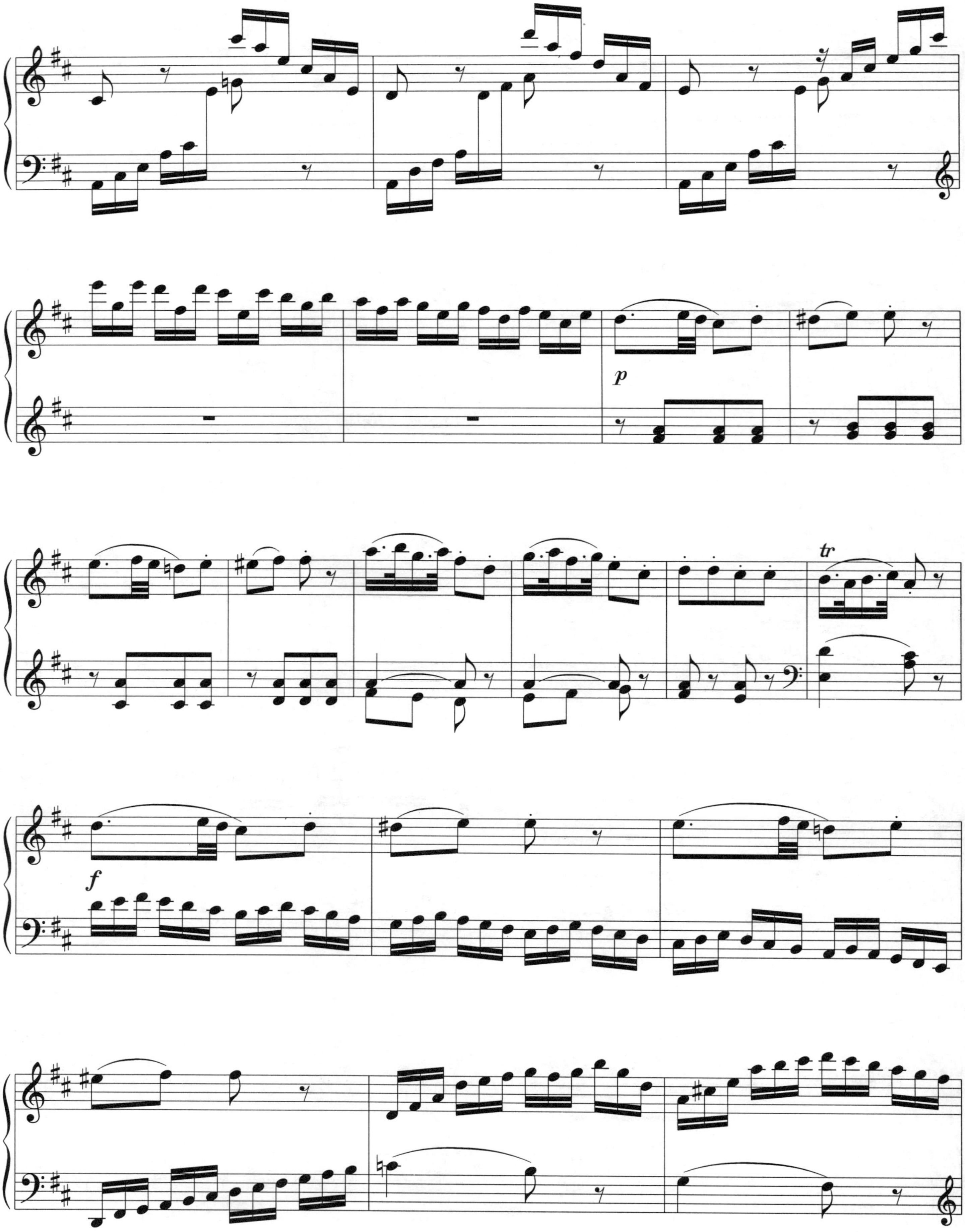
p
tr
f

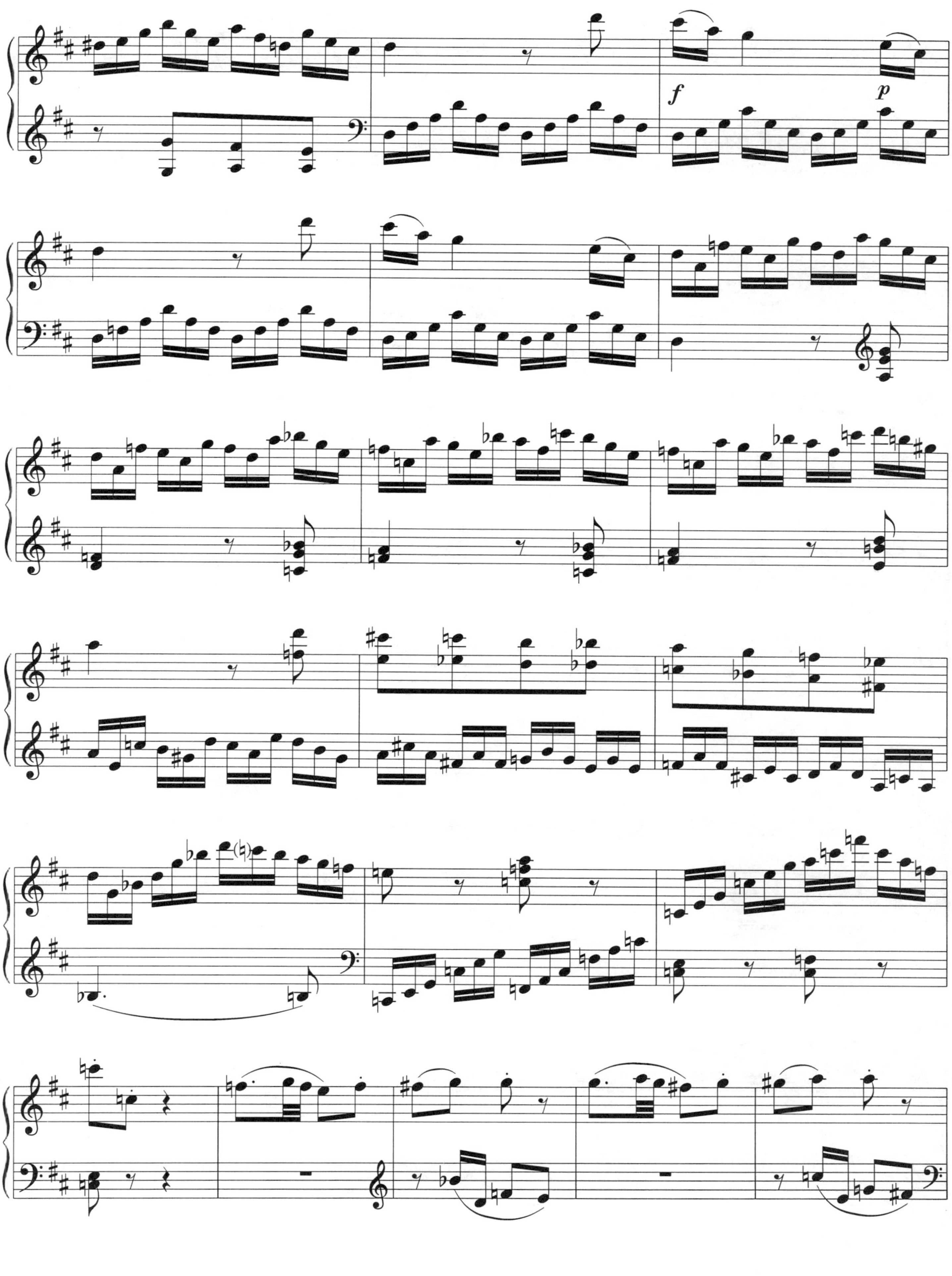
f
p

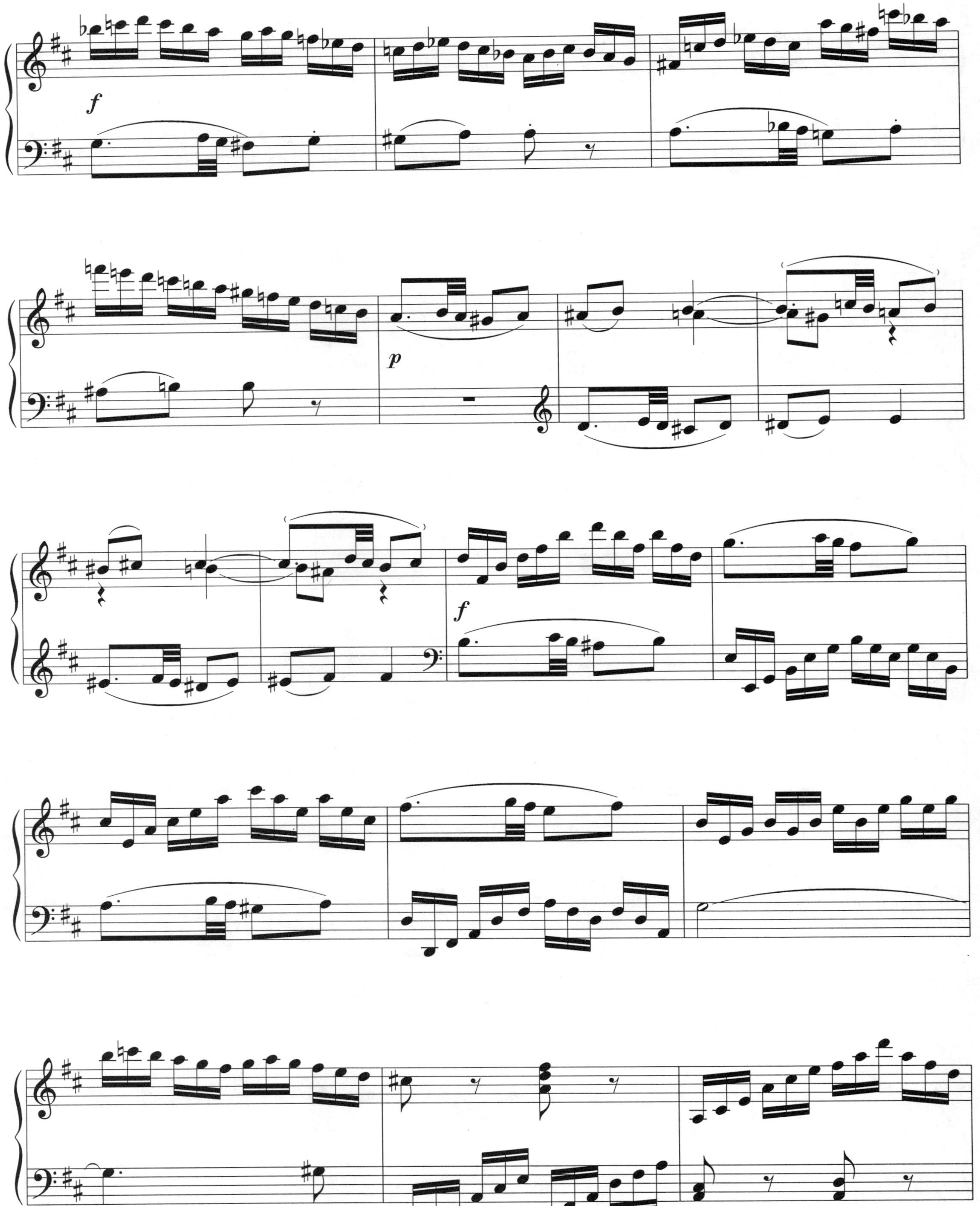
f
p
f

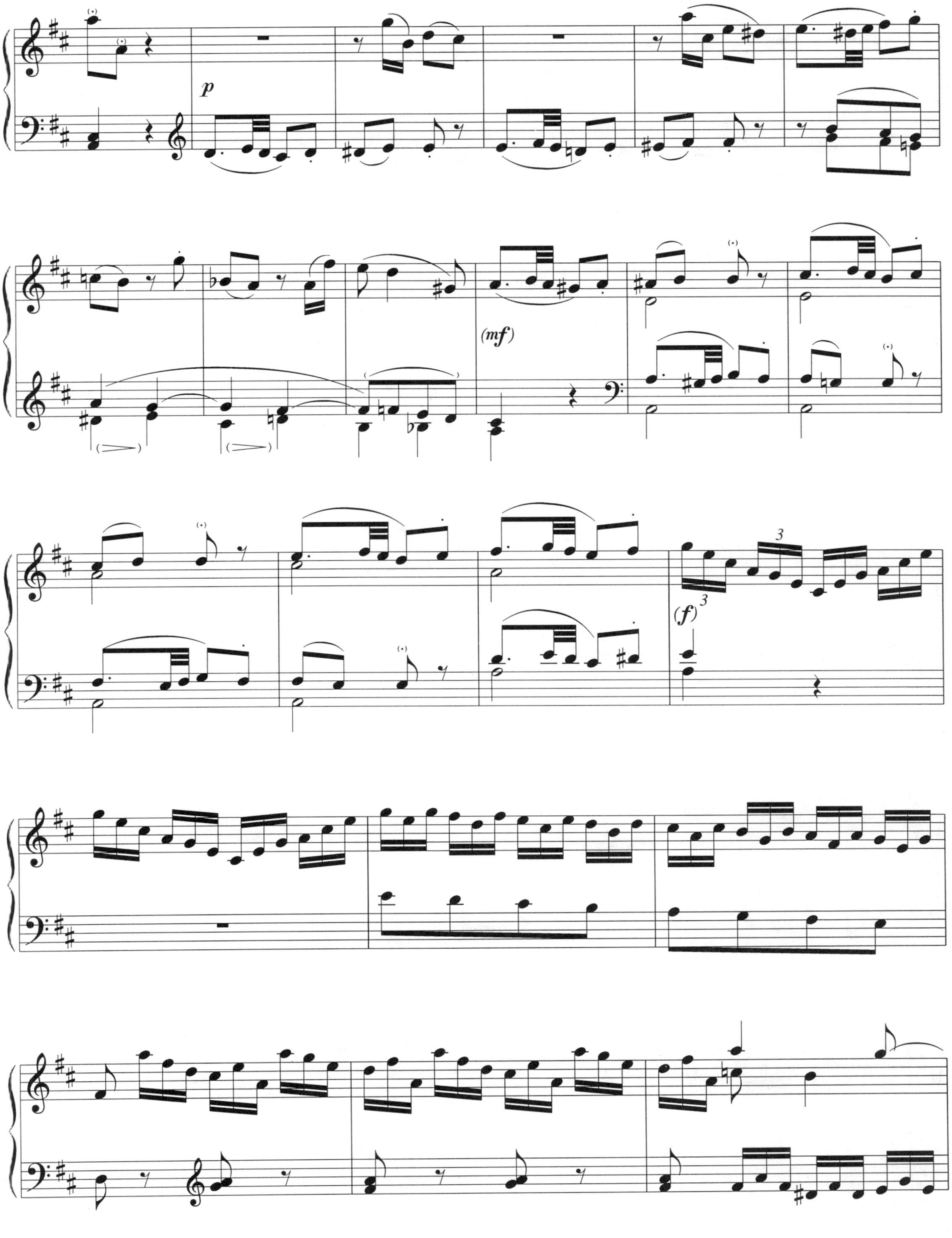
p
(mf)
(f)

70

71

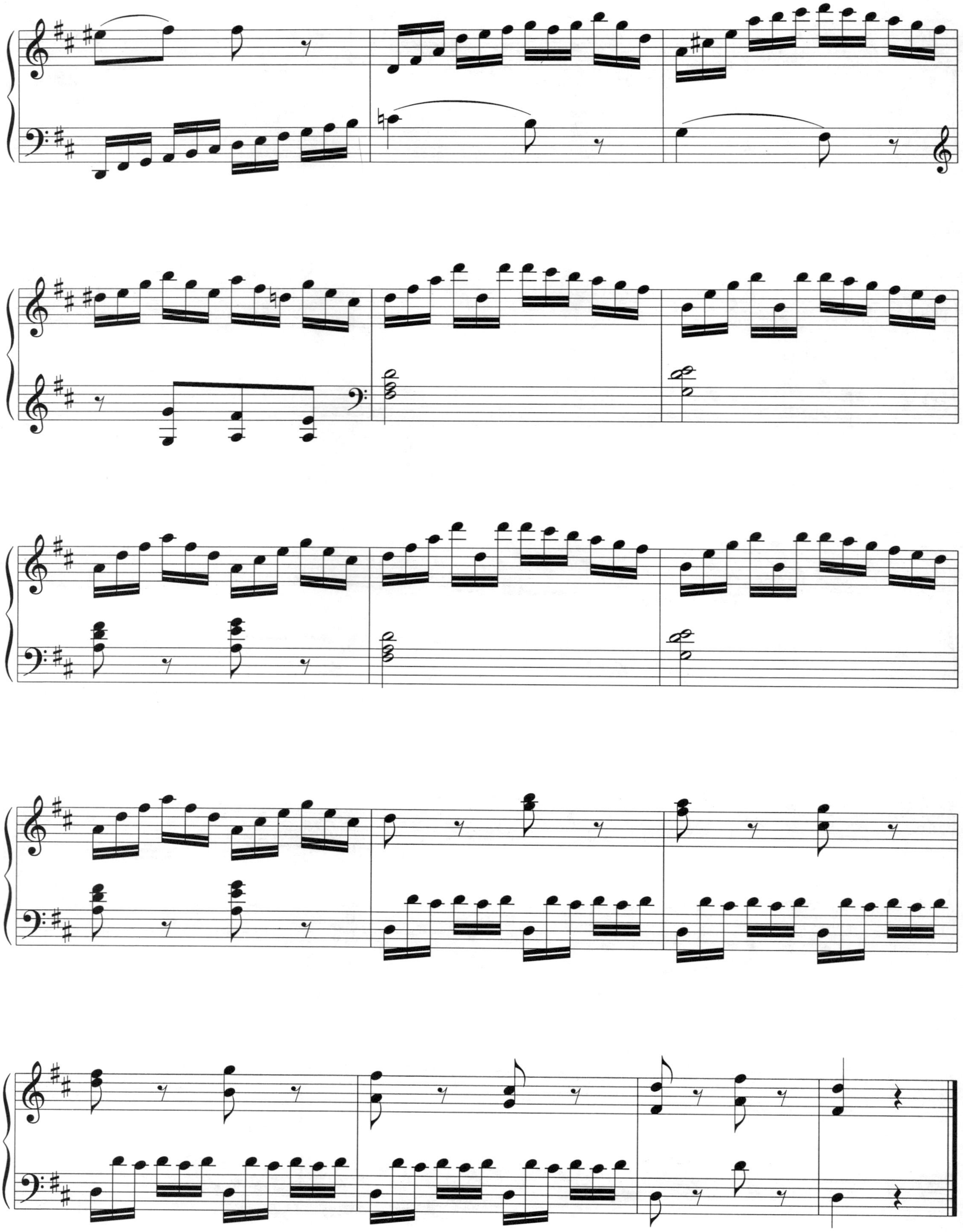

Jakob Ludwig Felix Mendelssohn
(November 3, 1809 - November 4, 1847)

Mendelssohn's father was a rich banker. All distinguished musicians passing through Berlin visited their home. On Sunday there was always an afternoon concert by Felix and his talented sister Fanny. Mendelssohn began to compose at the age of 10. He not only composed and performed his own works, but he also revived the works of Johann Sebastian Bach, which had been forgotten for a hundred years.

Sonata in G Minor
(Op. 105)

Felix Mendelssohn

Allegro

75

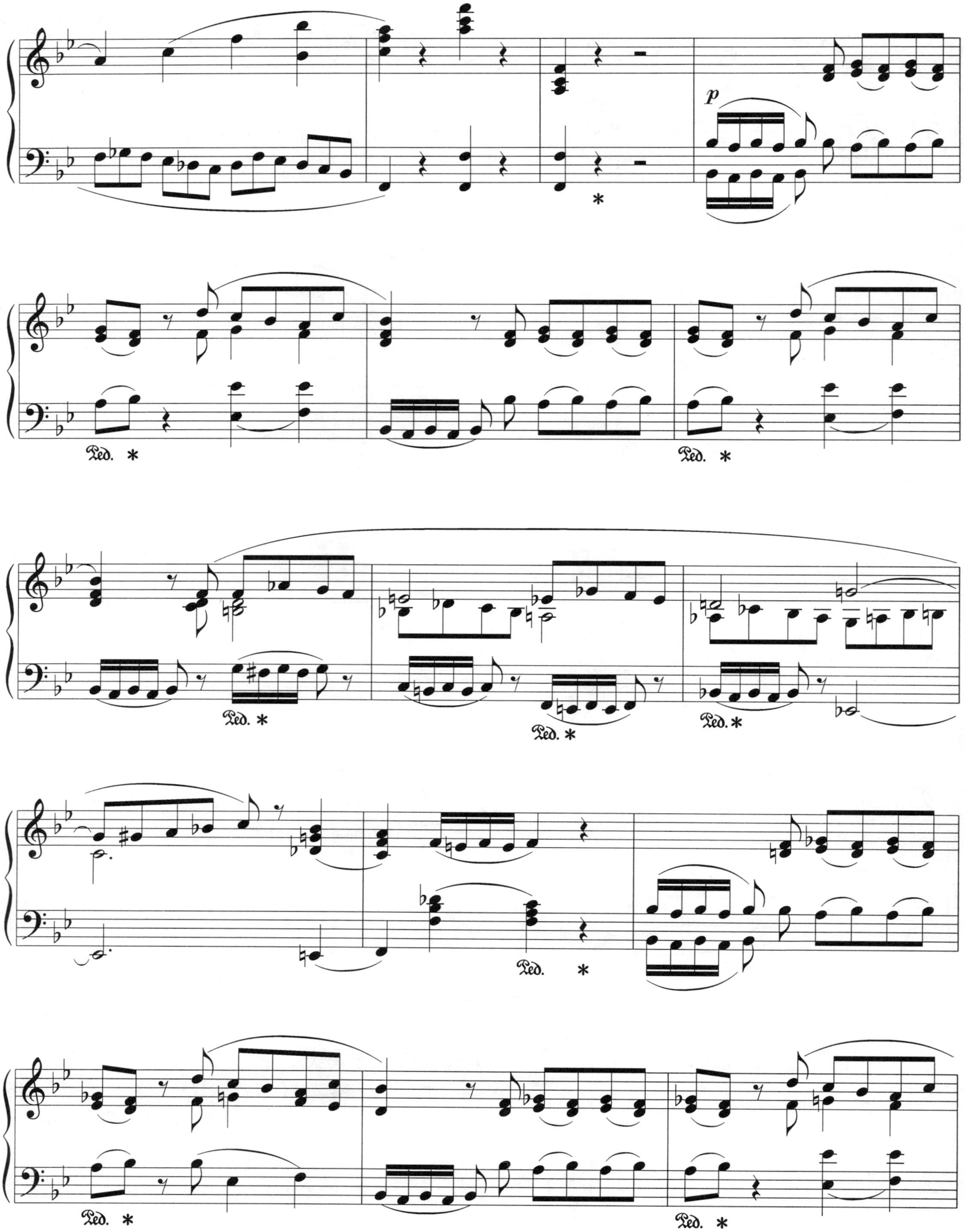
p
Ped.
Ped.
Ped.
Ped.
Ped.
Ped.
Ped.
Ped.

77

78

79

80

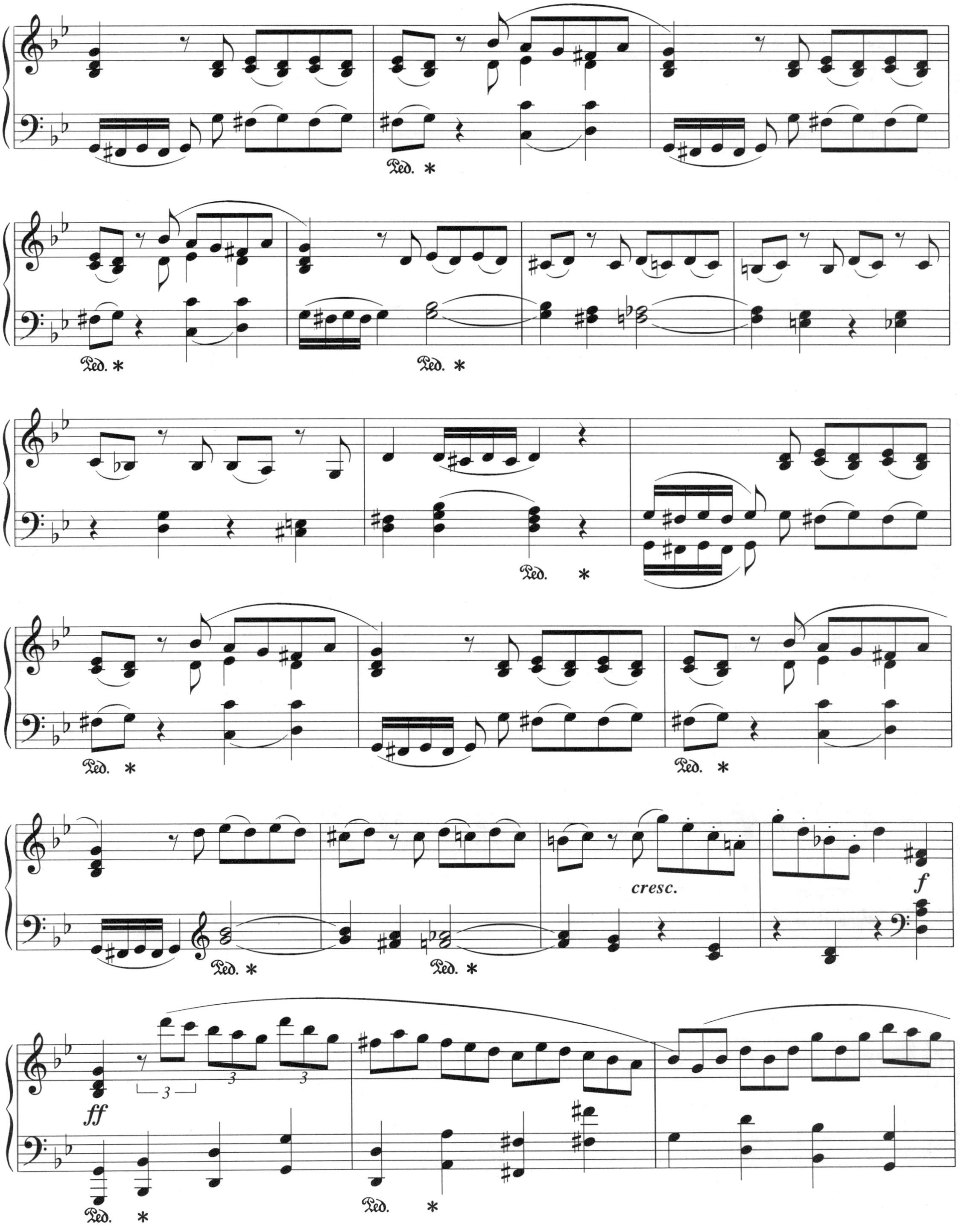
Ped.
cresc.
f
ff

82

83

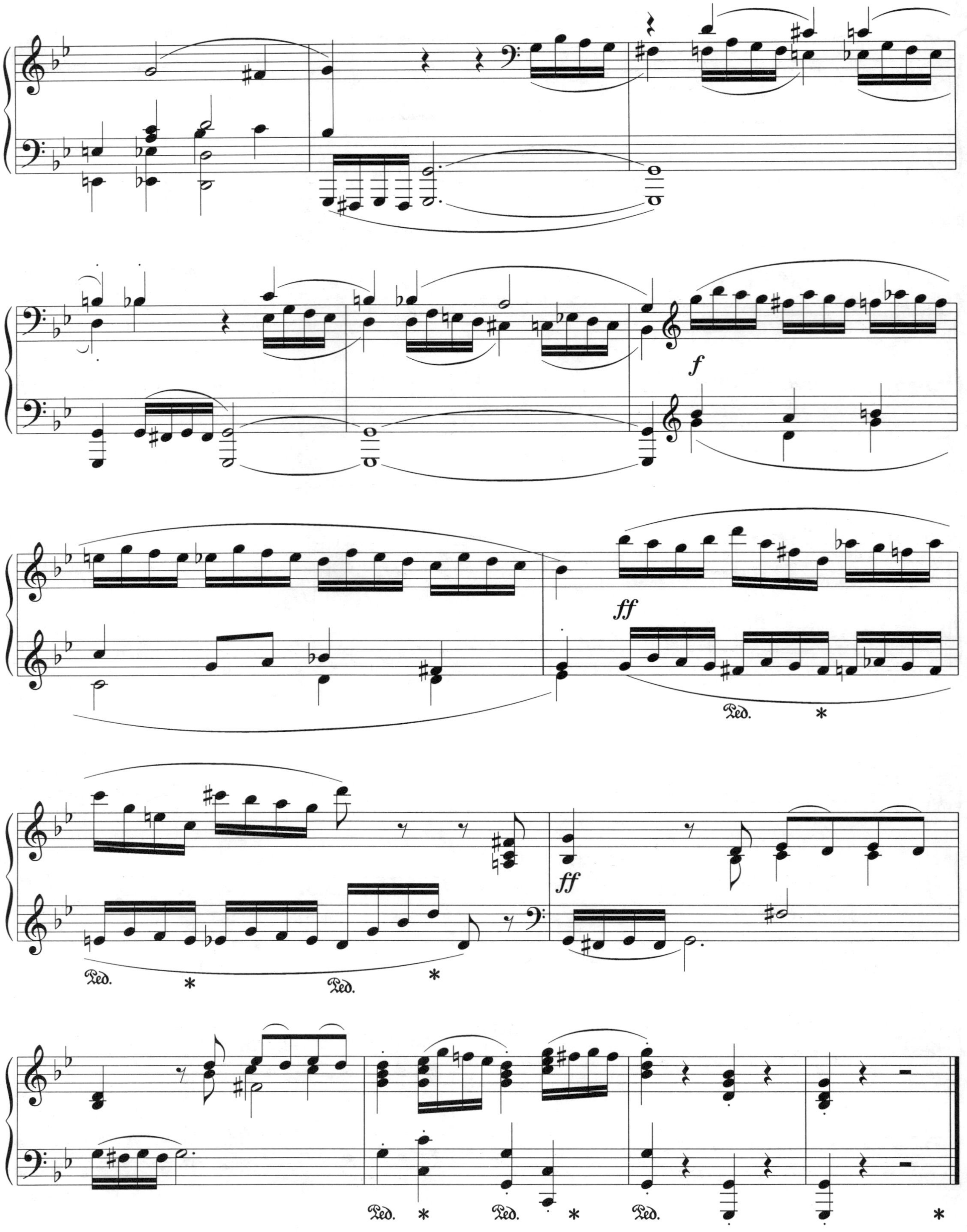
f
ff
Ped.
ff
Ped.
Ped.
Ped.
Ped.
Ped.

85

86

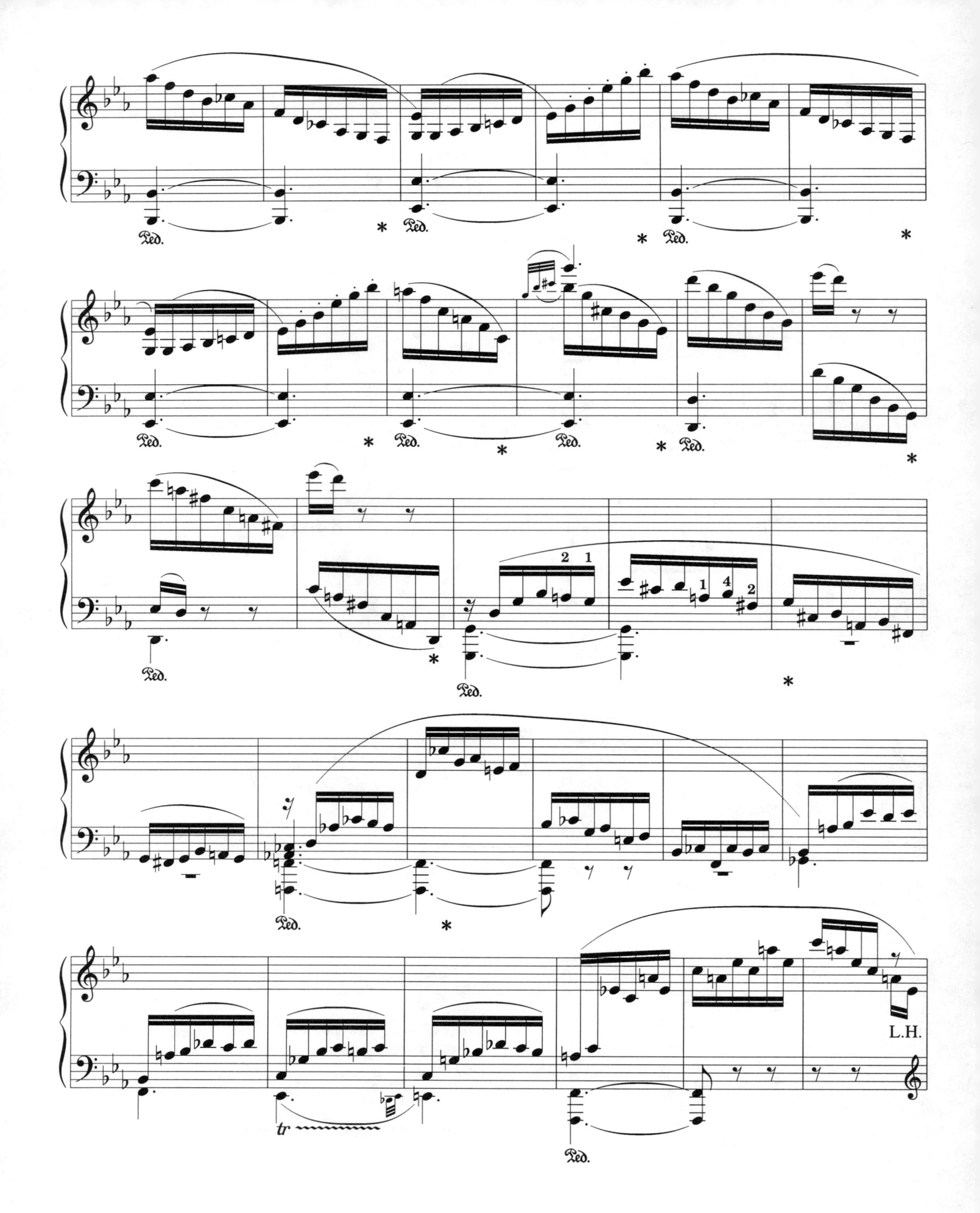

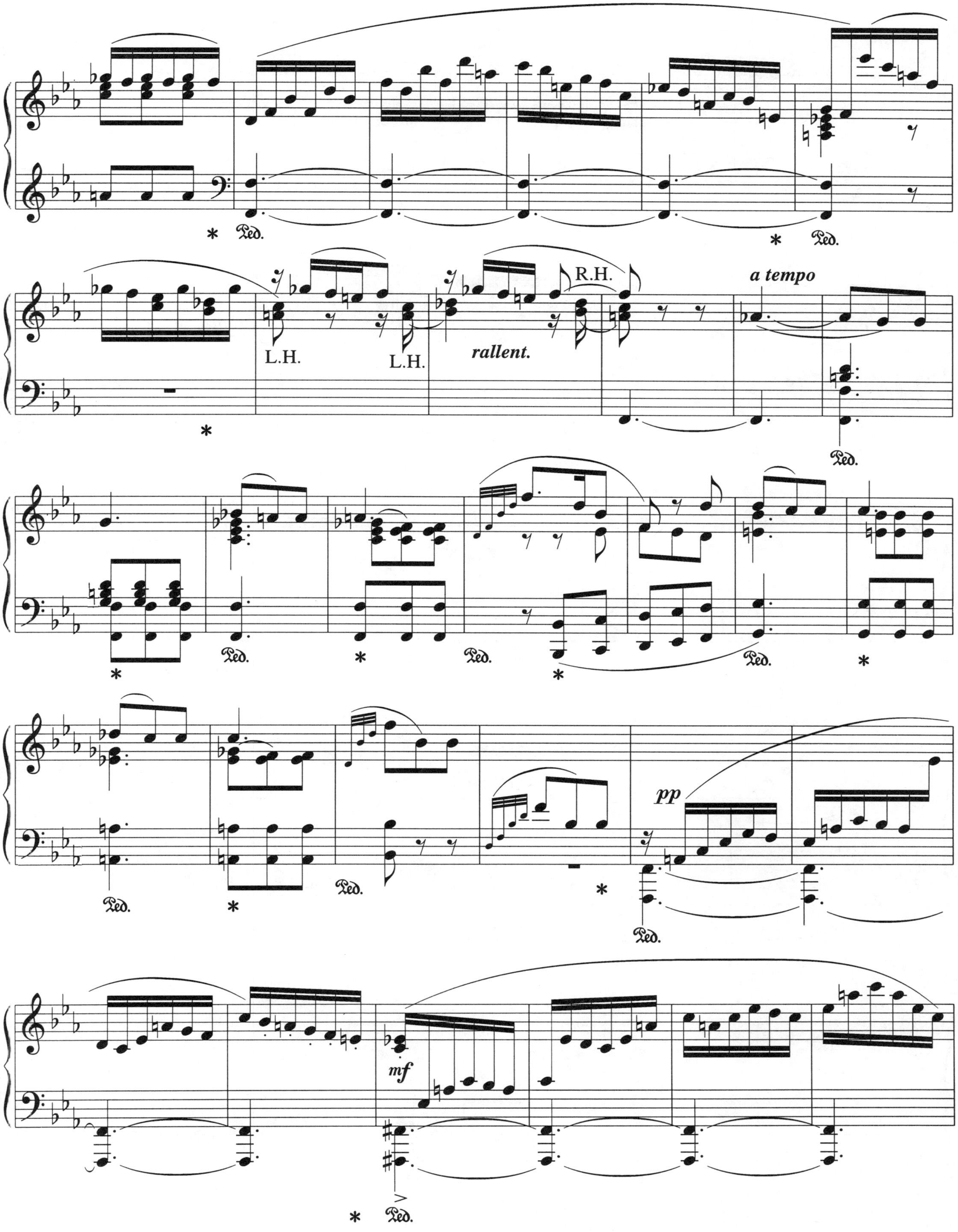
R.H.
a tempo
L.H.
L.H.
rallent.
pp
mf
Ped.

88

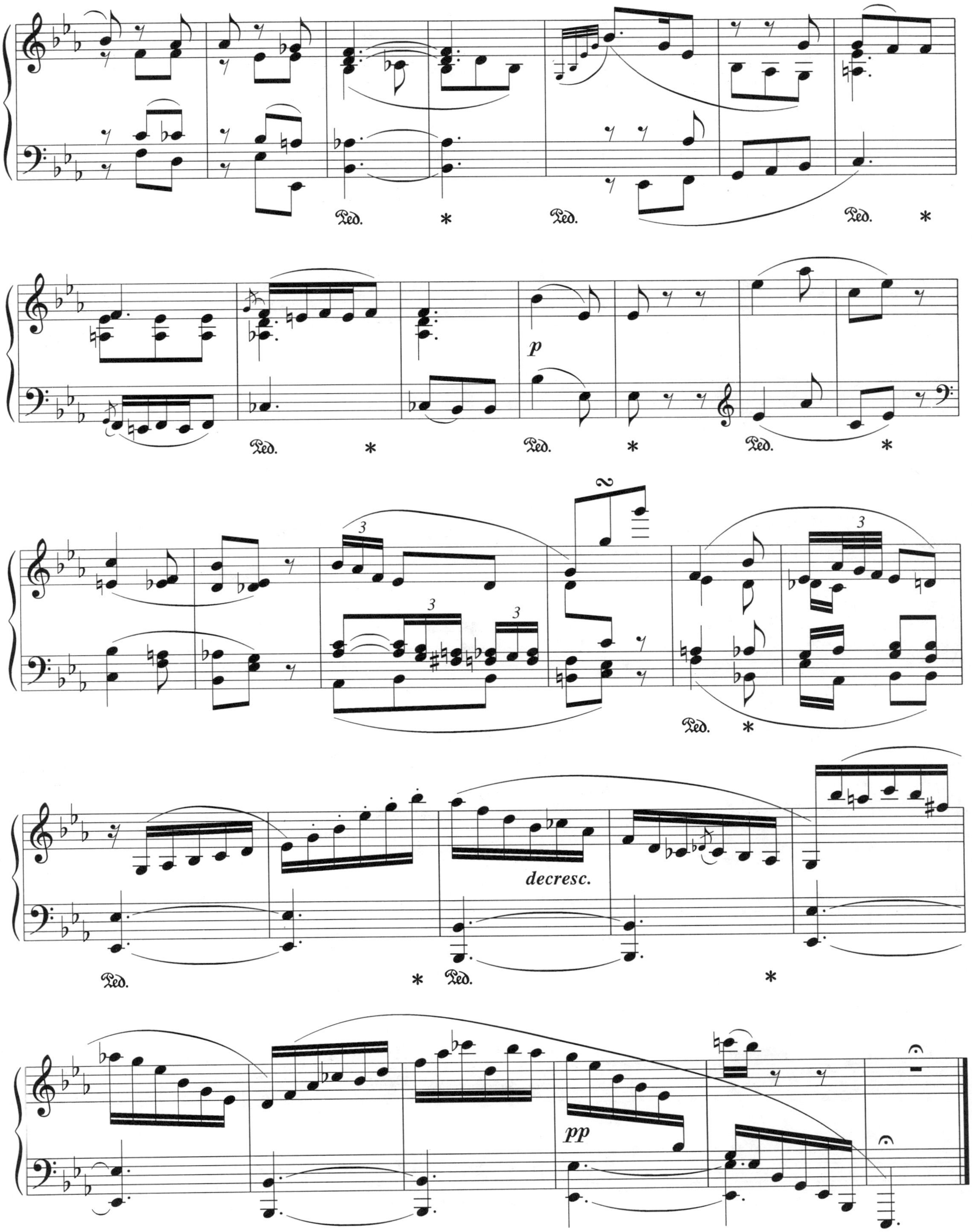

Ped.
*
Ped.
Ped.
*
Ped.
*
Ped.
*
p
Ped.
*
3
3
3
3
Ped.
*
decresc.
Ped.
*
Ped.
*
pp

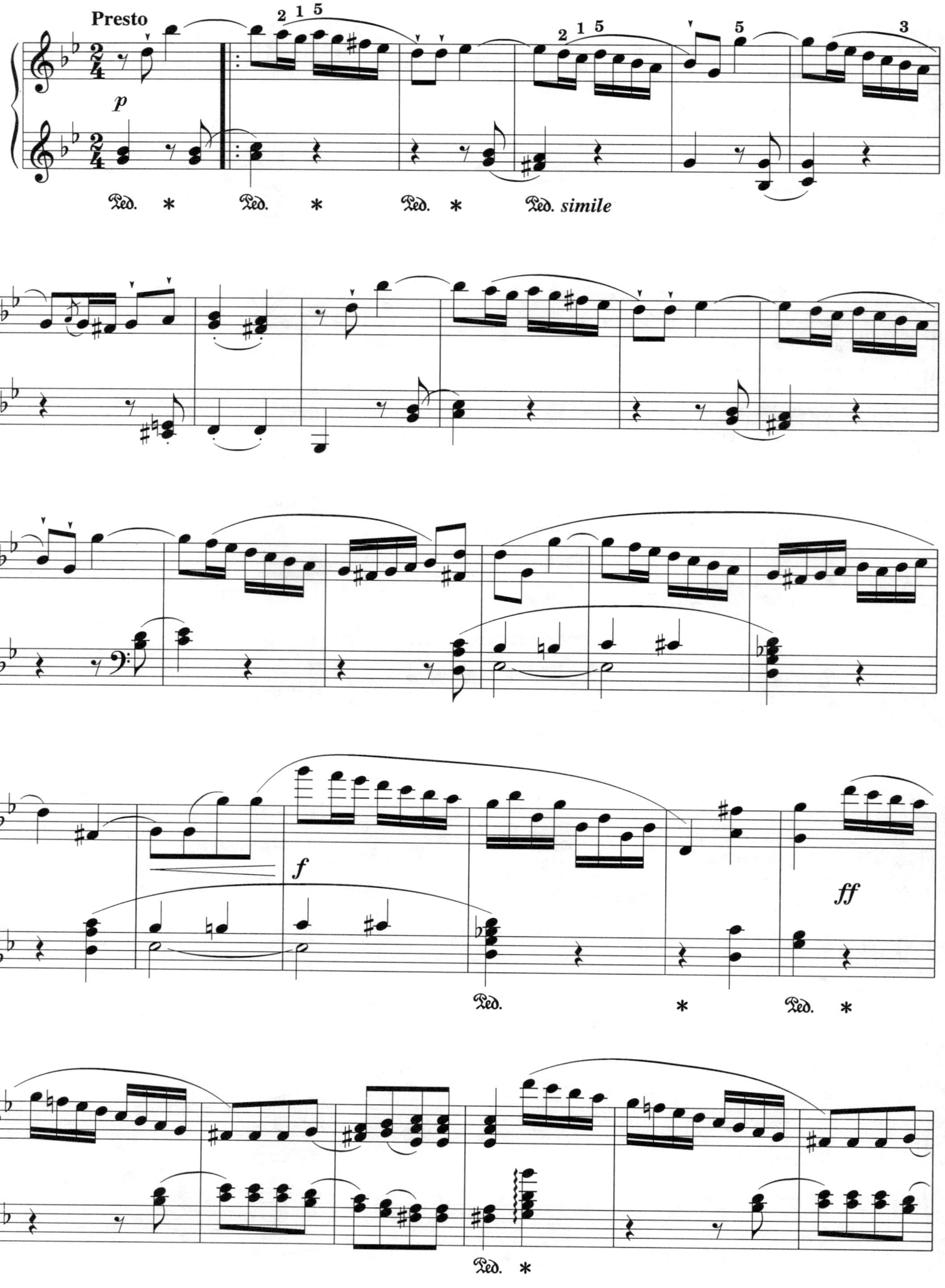
Presto
p
Ped. *
Ped. simile
f
ff

91

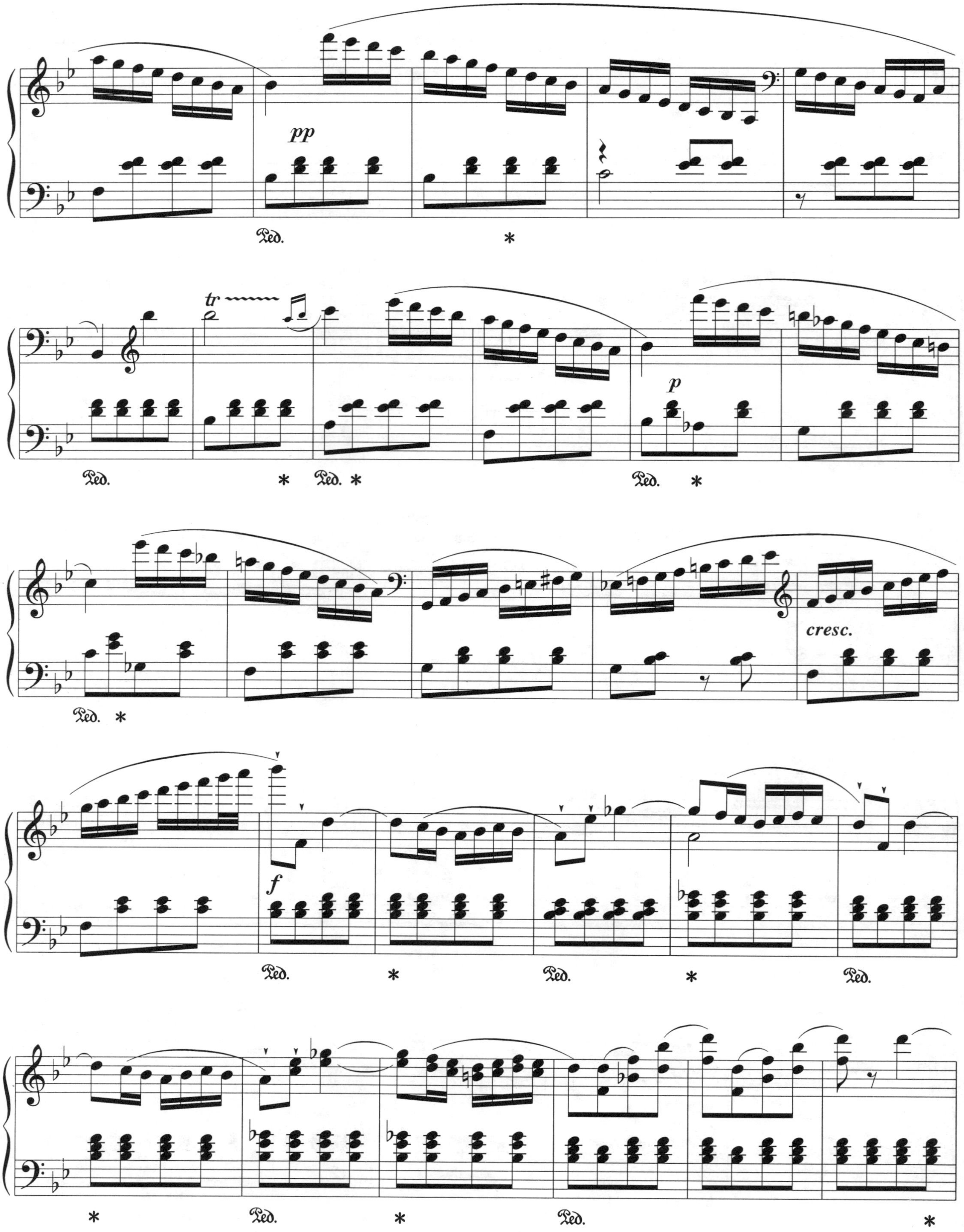
pp
Ped.
tr
p
cresc.
f

93

94

95

96

97

Franz Joseph Haydn
(March 31, 1732 – May 31, 1809)

Most of Haydn's life was spent working for Prince Esterhazy as his "in-house" composer. Haydn was in charge of rehearsals and concerts, weddings and royal visits. He also had to supervise the life and conduct of all the musicians working under him. Because Haydn was very isolated there, he was forced to be original. His fame spread, however, and Haydn's works became published in Paris and Amsterdam. Haydn was very industrious, working 16 hours a day, often working on several compositions at a time. He had a suite of three rooms in the palace. The palace contained 162 rooms, a white marble reception hall, splendid library, theatre, and opera-house, all royally decorated and lavishly furnished.

Sonata in E Minor

Joseph Haydn

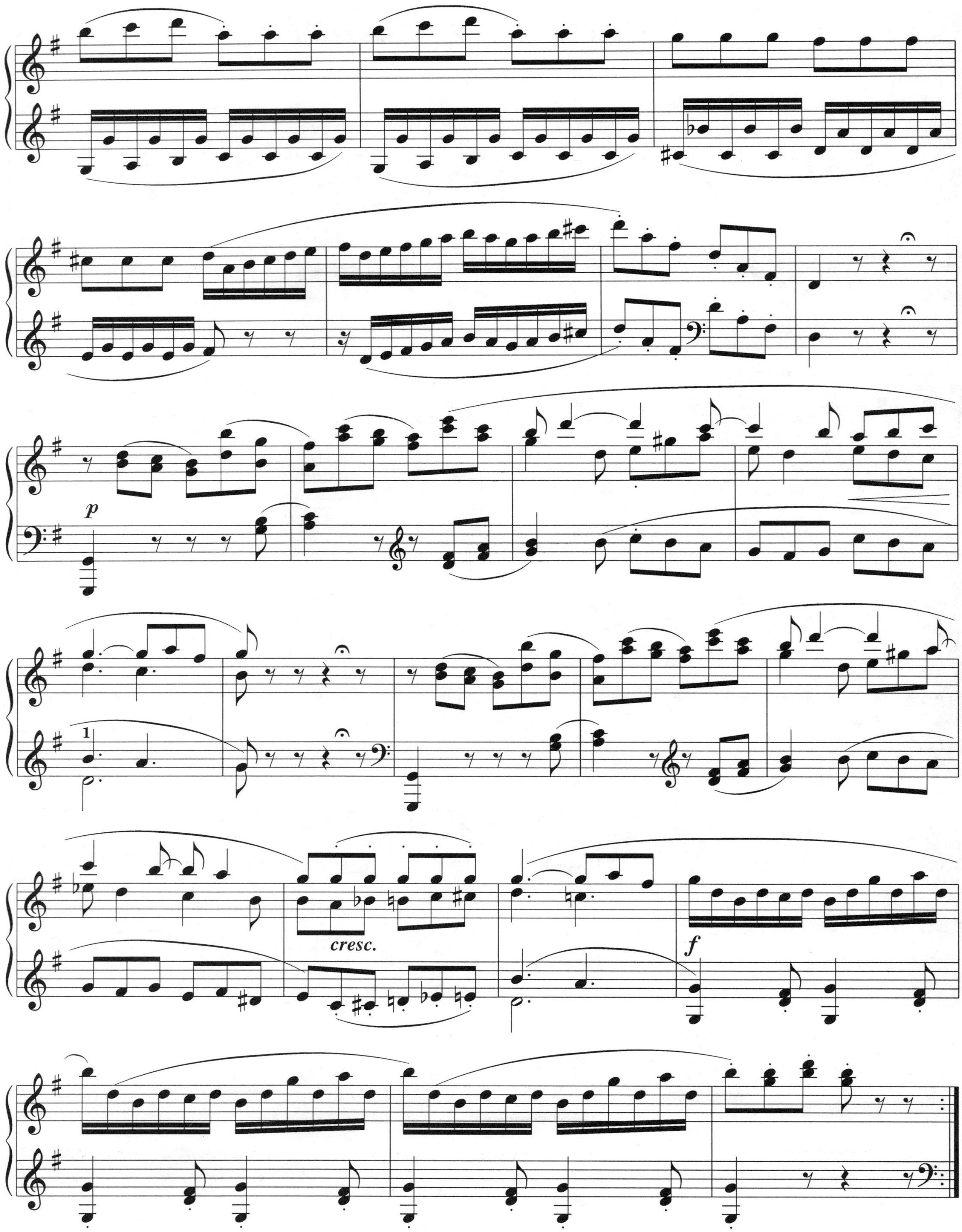
p
1
cresc.
f

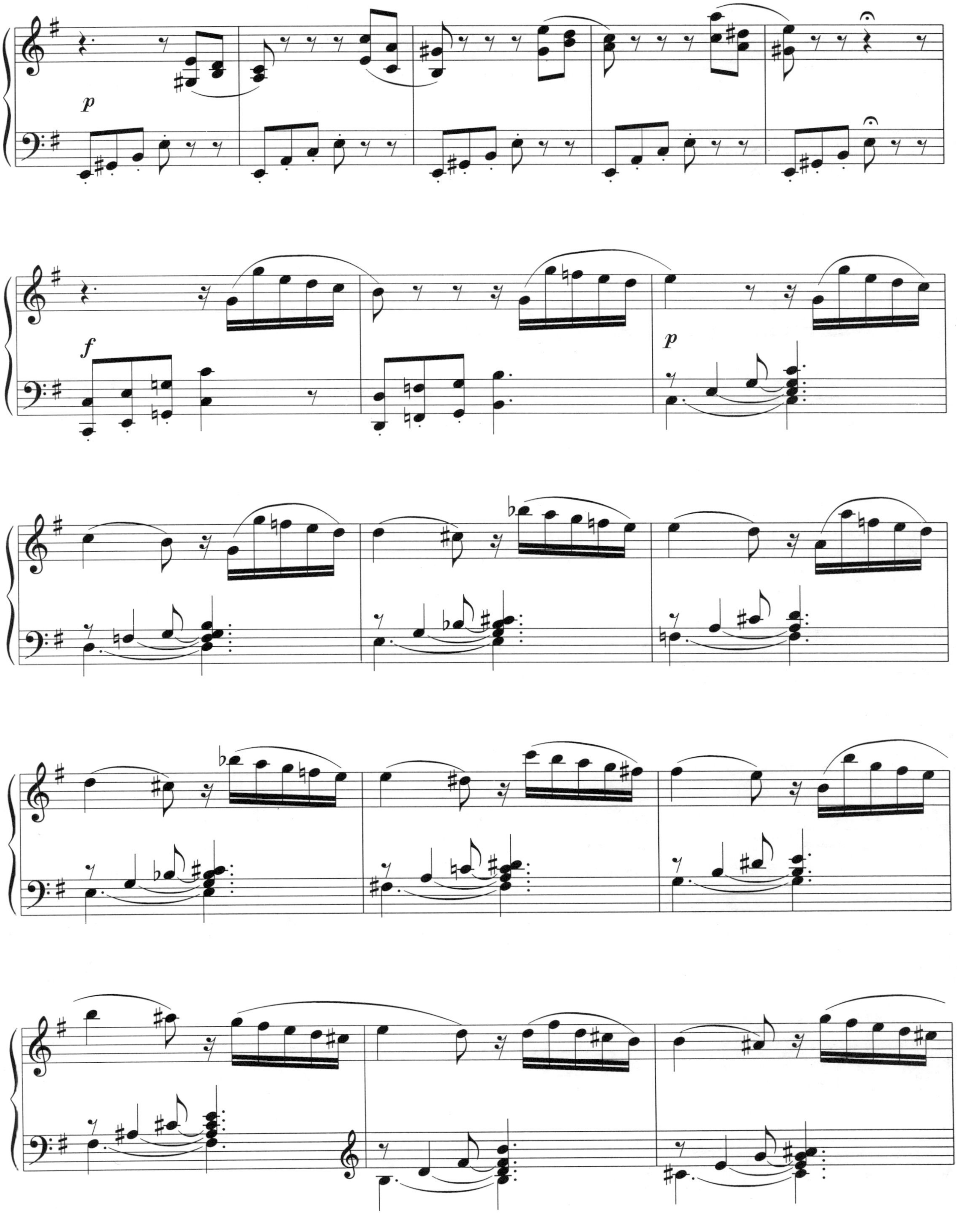
p
f
p

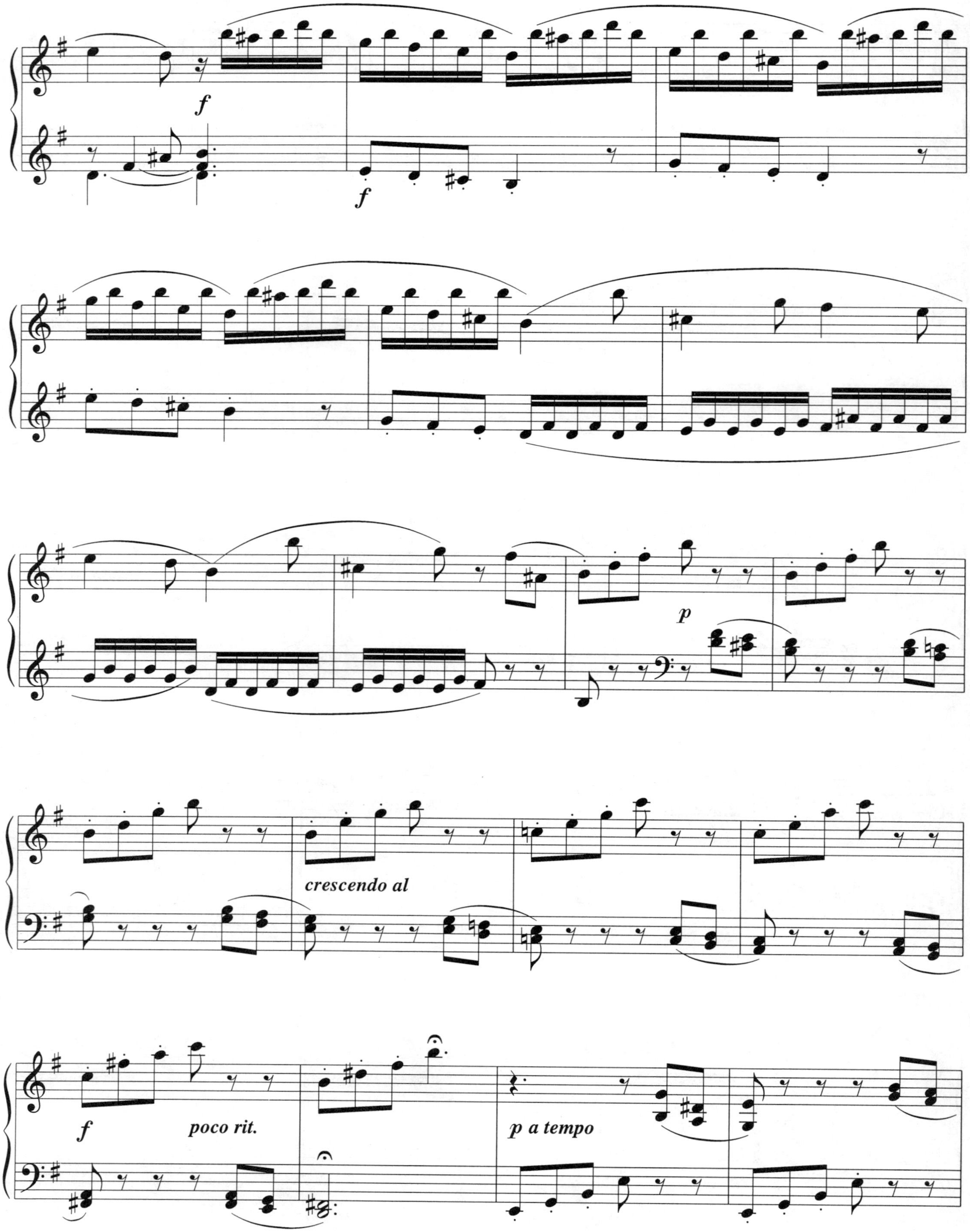
f
f
p
crescendo al
f
poco rit.
p a tempo

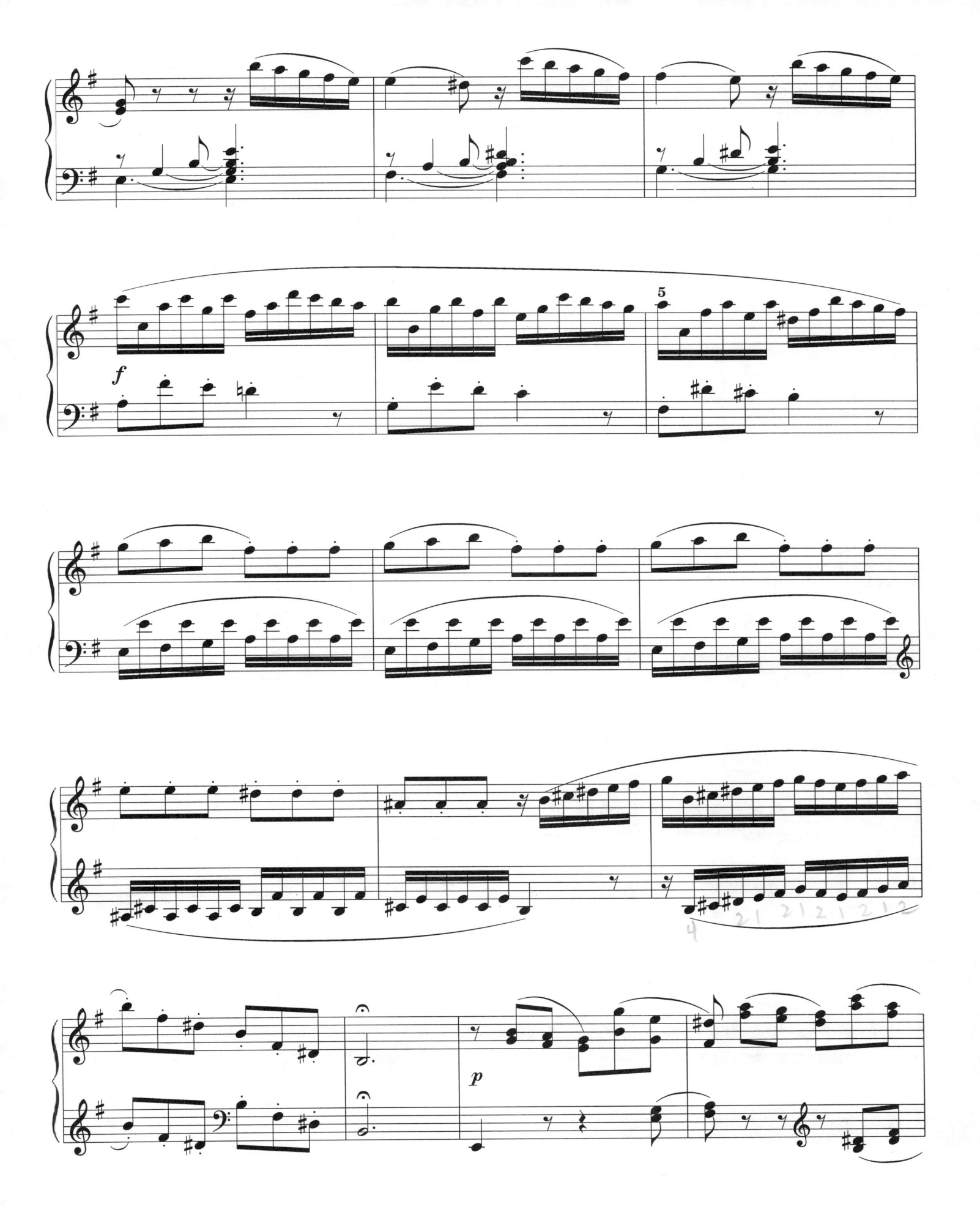
f
5
p

104

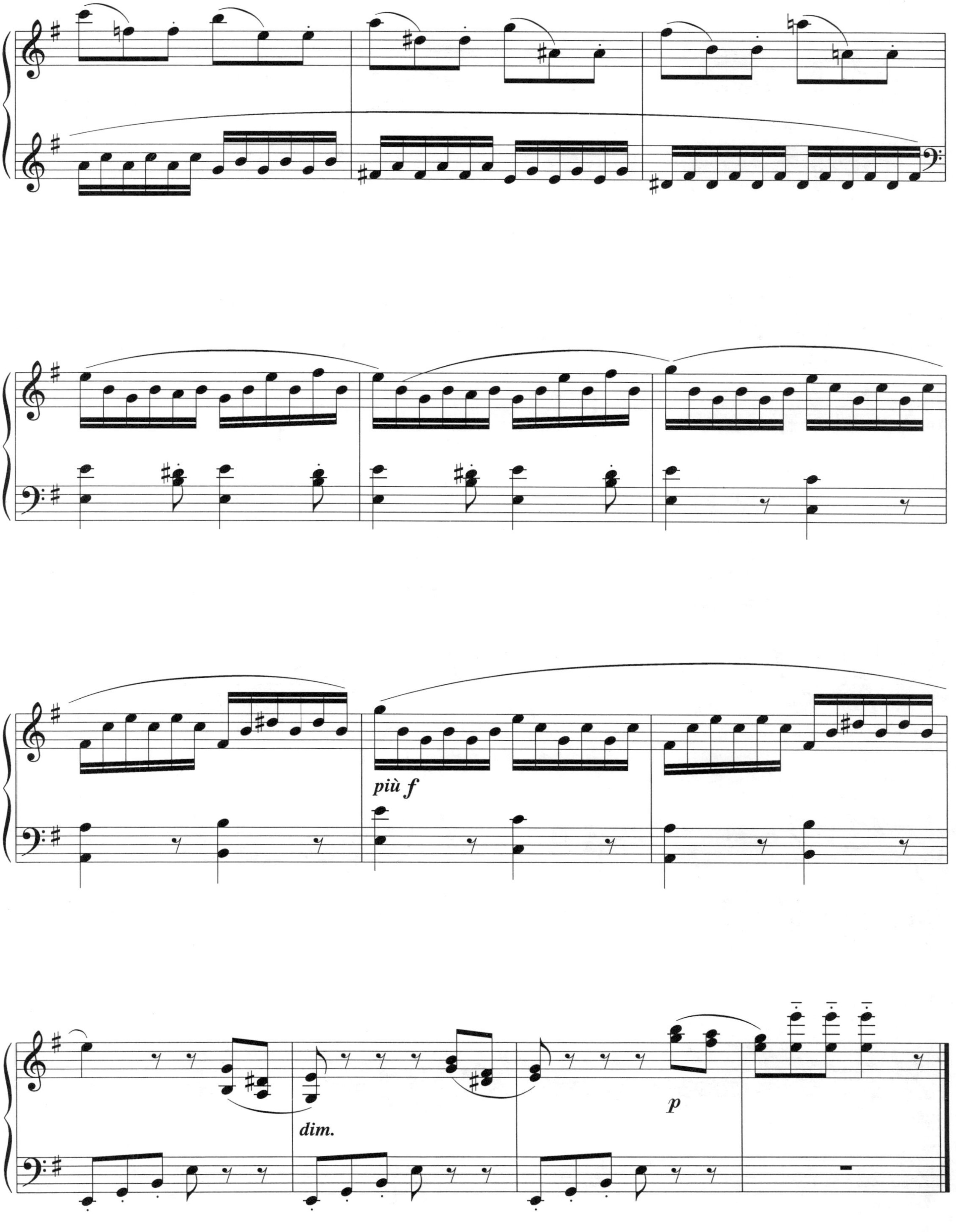
più f
dim.
p

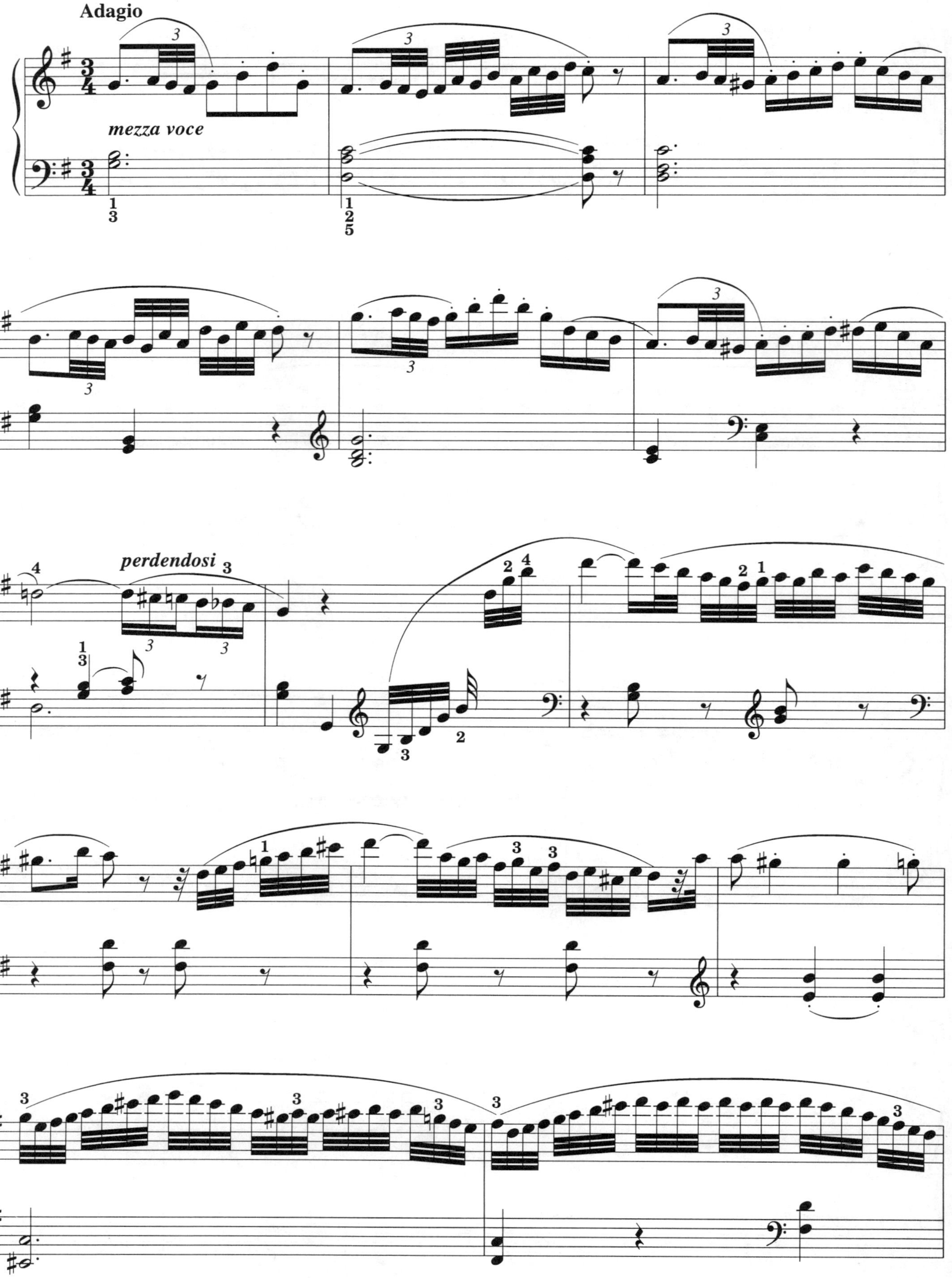

Adagio
mezza voce
perdendosi

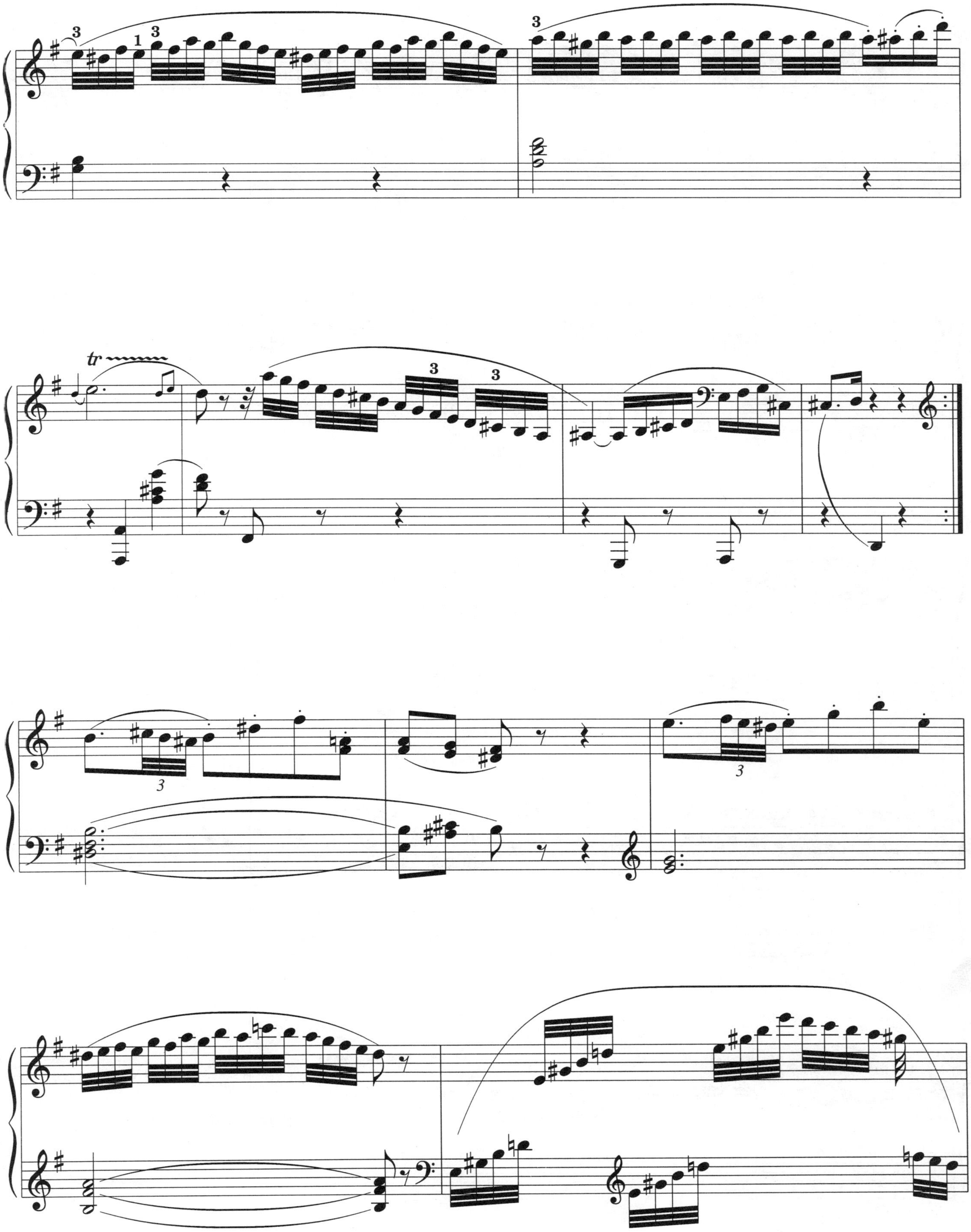
tr

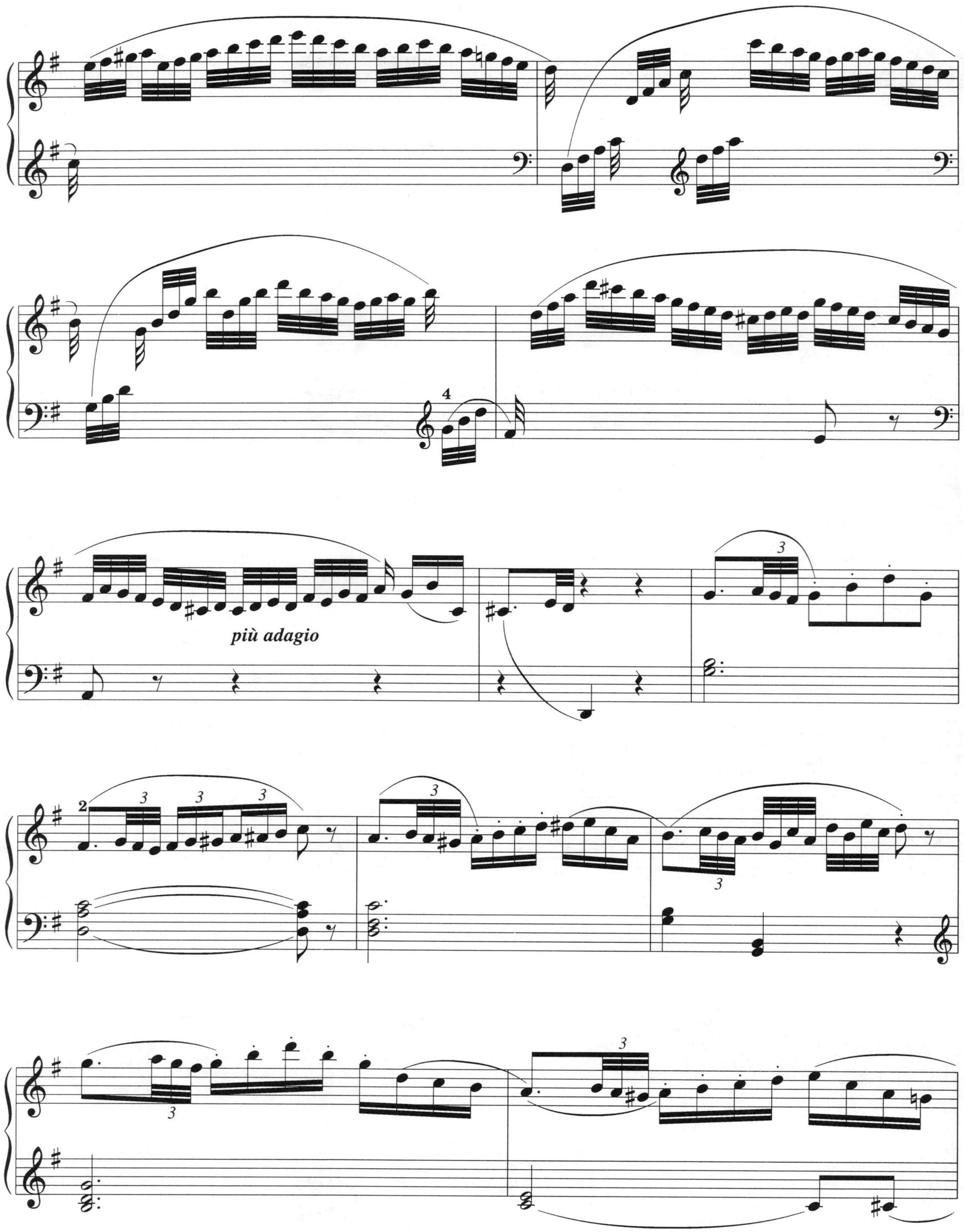
più adagio

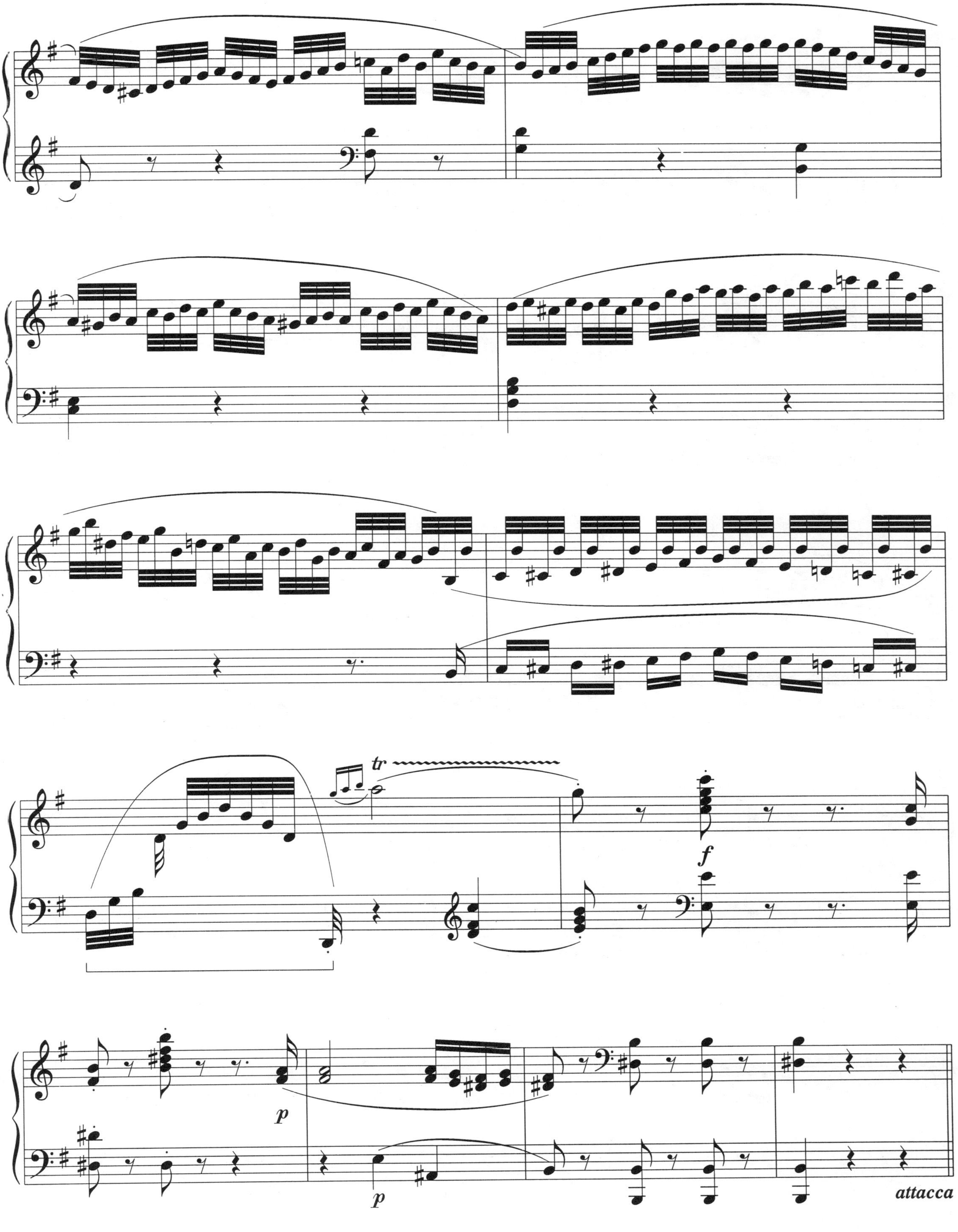
tr
f
p
p
attacca

Finale

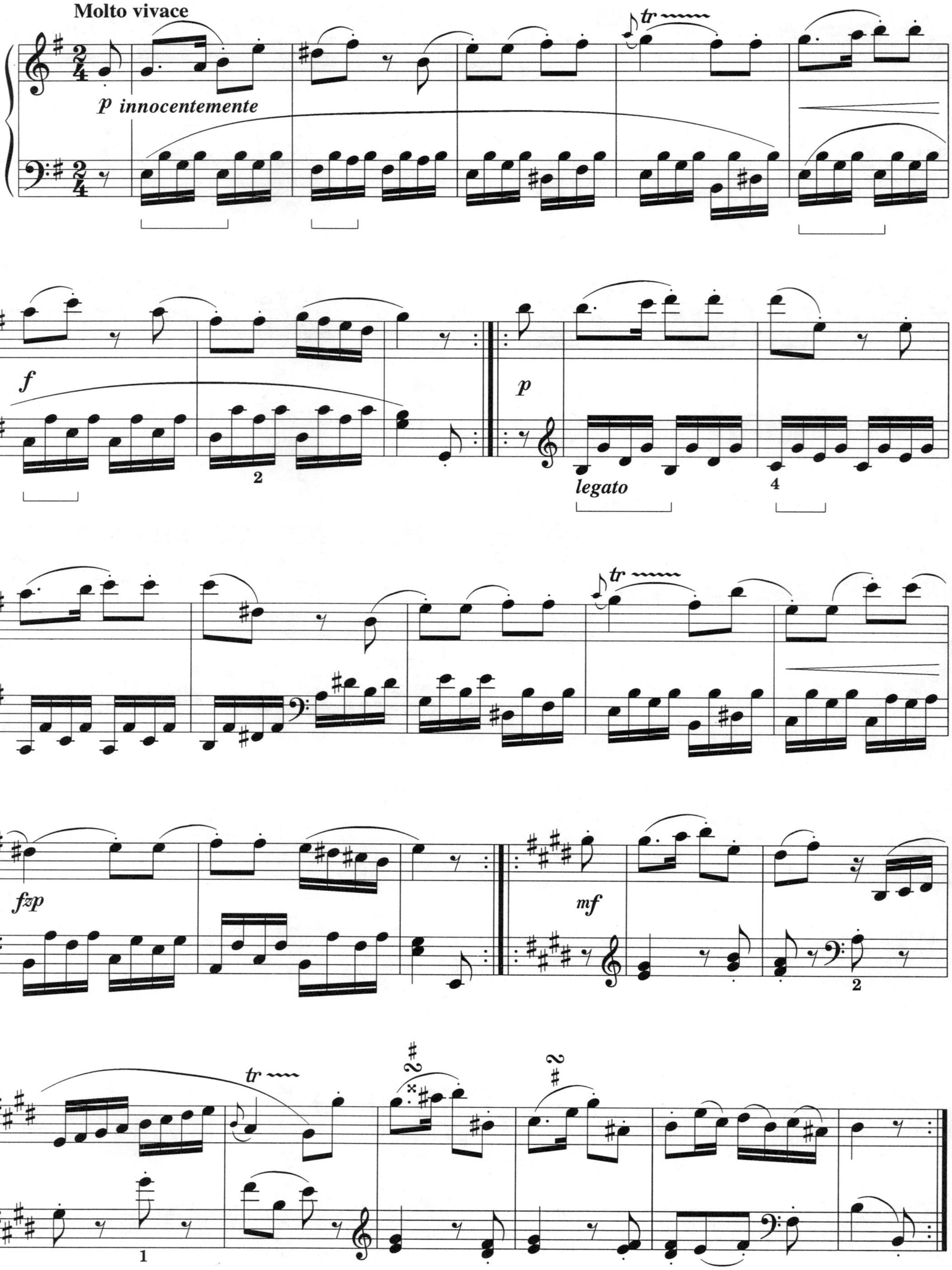

111

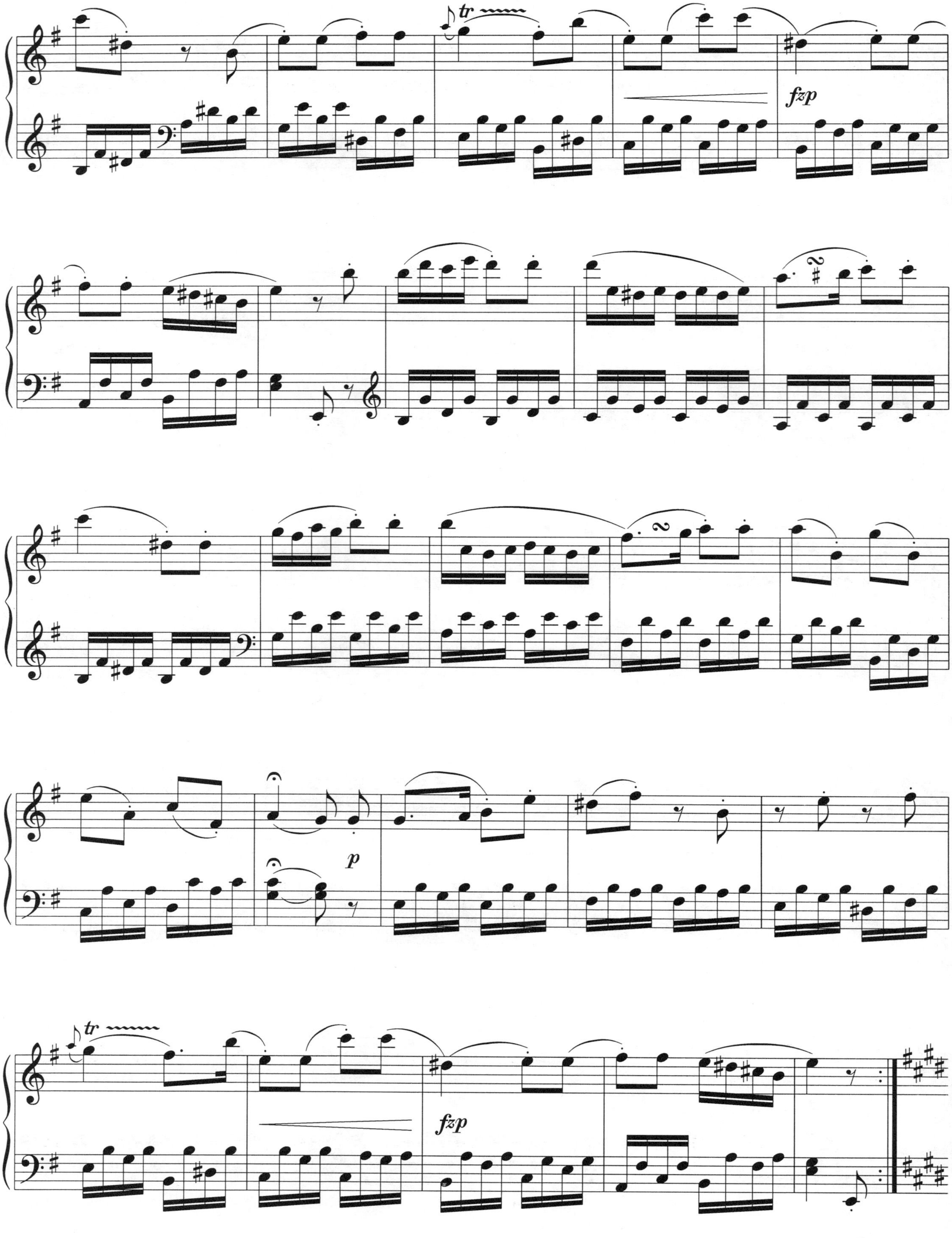

tr
fzp
p
tr
fzp

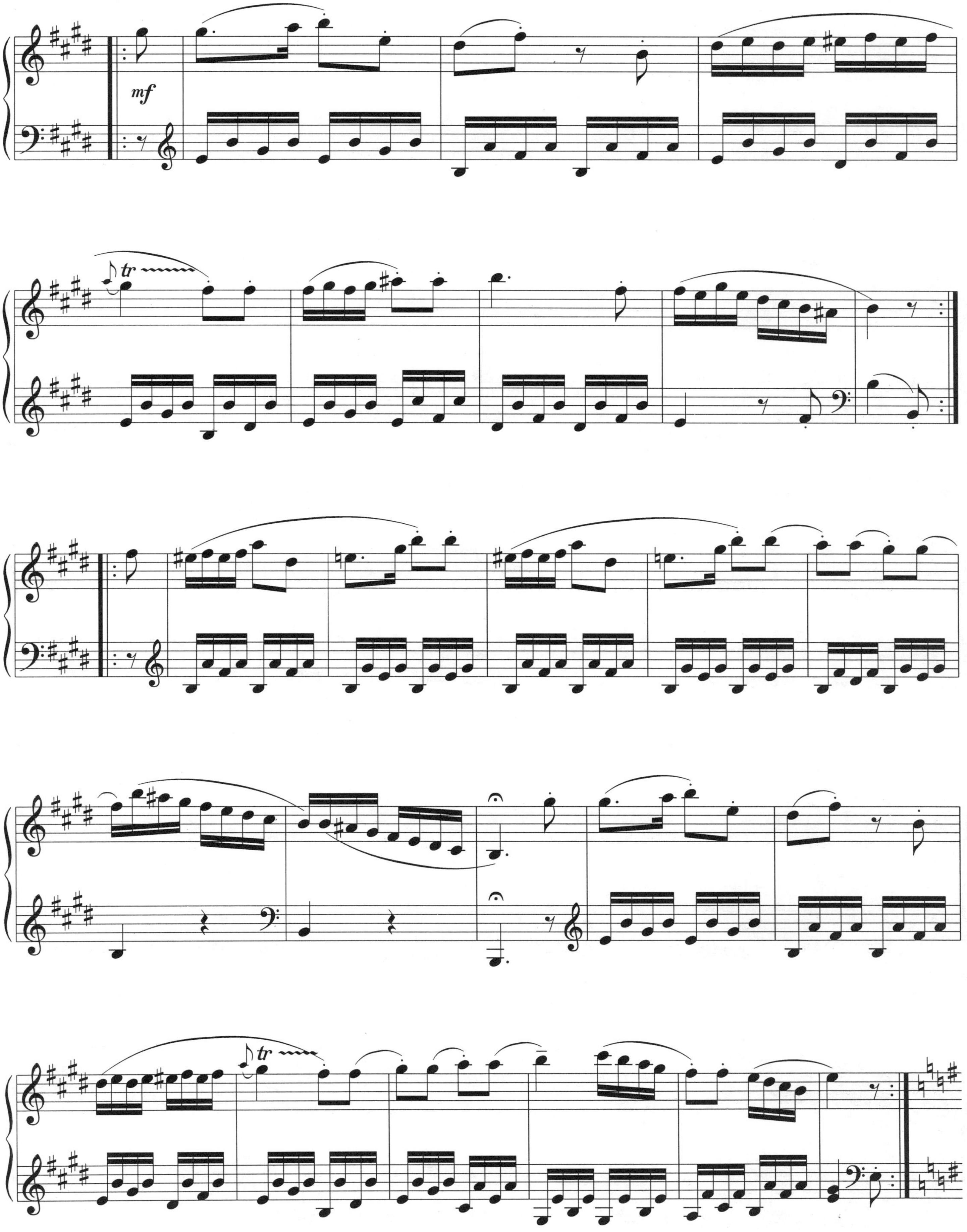
mf
tr
tr

114

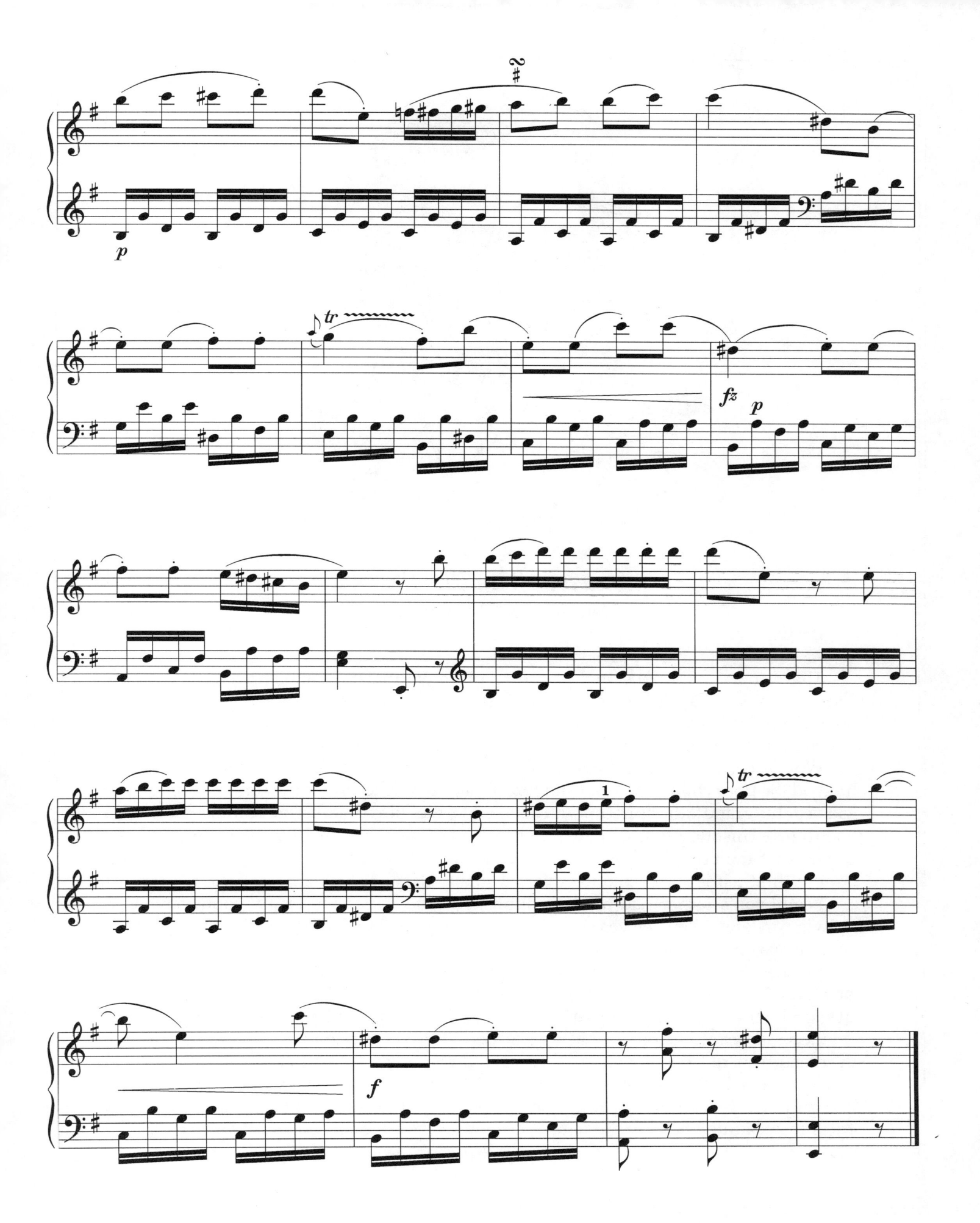
p
tr
fz
p
tr
f

Ludwig Van Beethoven
(December 17, 1770 - March 26, 1827)

Beethoven!

That name stands alone on the pedestal of a memorial monument in the city of Bonn, Germany. Bonn was Beethoven's birthplace. He was born there on December 17, 1770. Beethoven didn't know his correct age until he was forty because his father, wanting to exploit him as a child prodigy, always represented him as two years younger than he was.

When Beethoven was nine years old his father came home drunk one evening and dragged the poor child out of bed and forced him to practice the piano until morning. The next year his grandfather's friend Van den Eeden, the court organist, gave him lessons; and when he died his successor, Christian Gottlob Neefe, took charge of him. Beethoven learned so well that the boy, then just eleven and a half, served as deputy organist during his absence (first without pay and later with a small salary).

Beethoven's father had already published nine variations by "a young amateur, Ludwig van Beethoven, ten years old" (he was really twelve). He stopped attending school when he was thirteen years old.

In the spring of 1787, Beethoven went to Vienna and studied composition with Mozart and studied counterpoint with Haydn. However, his hope of studying on with Mozart was cut short by the news of his mother's failing health. He returned quickly to Bonn. She died and the same year his little sister Margaret died. This was no doubt a very sad time for the seventeen-year-old Beethoven and, to make matters worse, his father continued to get drunk to the point that Beethoven occasionally had to rescue his father from the hands of the police. In November 1789, just shy of being nineteen years of age, Beethoven was officially appointed head of the family, empowered to receive his father's salary.

In 1792, Beethoven returned to Vienna and became court organist. He kept a diary, so we know what he spent for boots, an overcoat, a piano, and rent. He was barely settled when news came of his father's sudden death by his own hand.

In the eight years ending with 1802 there were ninety-two compositions, including his thirty-two piano sonatas. In 1803 he exclaimed, "I am dissatisfied with my previous works; from today forth I am going to strike out into a new path."

Speaking to his friend Czerny he said, "I have never thought of writing for fame and honor. What is in my heart must out, and so I write."

He would hold an audience in his spell for hours with his improvisations reducing his listeners to tears, as Czerny relates, with the intensity of emotions he evoked.

While his deafness caused him to fall aloof from his friends and prevented him from making long tours that he had planned, it shut him into the realm of higher harmonies. He kept conversation books for use when he talked with friends and visitors. One hundred and thirty-six of the books are preserved in Berlin (covering the years between 1819 and 1827).

When his eldest brother died in 1815, Beethoven became stepfather to the nine-year-old Karl. This nephew gave him nothing but trouble the rest of his life. During the first five years of guardianship Beethoven seems to have composed only one solitary piece!

When Beethoven did compose, he was known to pour cold water over his hands and often times people below him complained of the water that soaked through his floor. It was also his habit to rise at daybreak, work until two or three, then have breakfast, and then spend the afternoon in the open air no matter what the weather was. He loved to wander for hours in the woods.

Beethoven died on the afternoon of March 26, 1827, during a heavy thunderstorm. Among the last to call upon him was Schubert. Schubert's friend, the composer Huttenbrenner, was with him when he died. The funeral attracted great attention. The schools were given a holiday to attend. More than two hundred carriages and thirty thousand pedestrians took part in the funeral procession. The coffin was carried by eight musicians. Mozart's *Requiem Mass* was sung in the Augustinian parish church.

The music of Beethoven makes a powerful and lasting impression. He was the real musical giant of the nineteenth century.

Sonata Pathétique
(Op. 13)

Ludwig van Beethoven

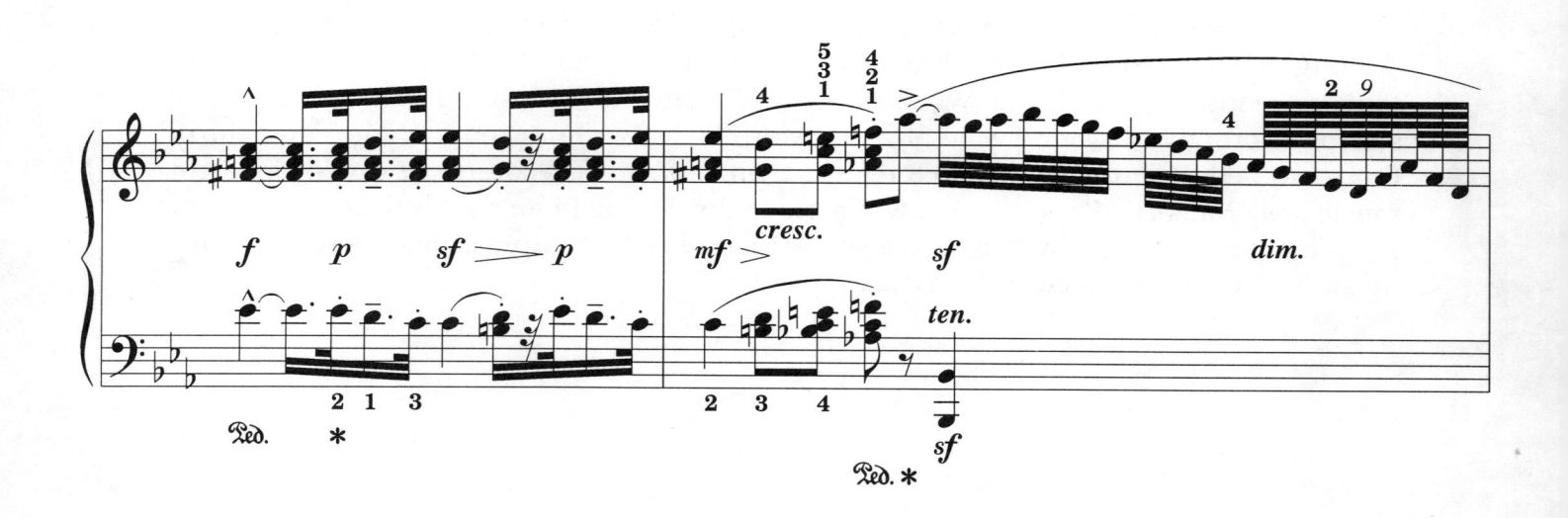

119

Allegro di molto e con brio (𝅗𝅥 = 144)
ten.
a)
p
sf
p
cresc.
dim.
ten.
p
sf
p
cresc.
dim.
agitato
p
sf
sf
sf
Ped.
*

121

122

sf
dolce
poco cresc.
decresc.
(poco slentando, ma poco)
pp
(a tempo) legato
Ped.
meno legato
cresc.

124

125

Allegro molto e con brio

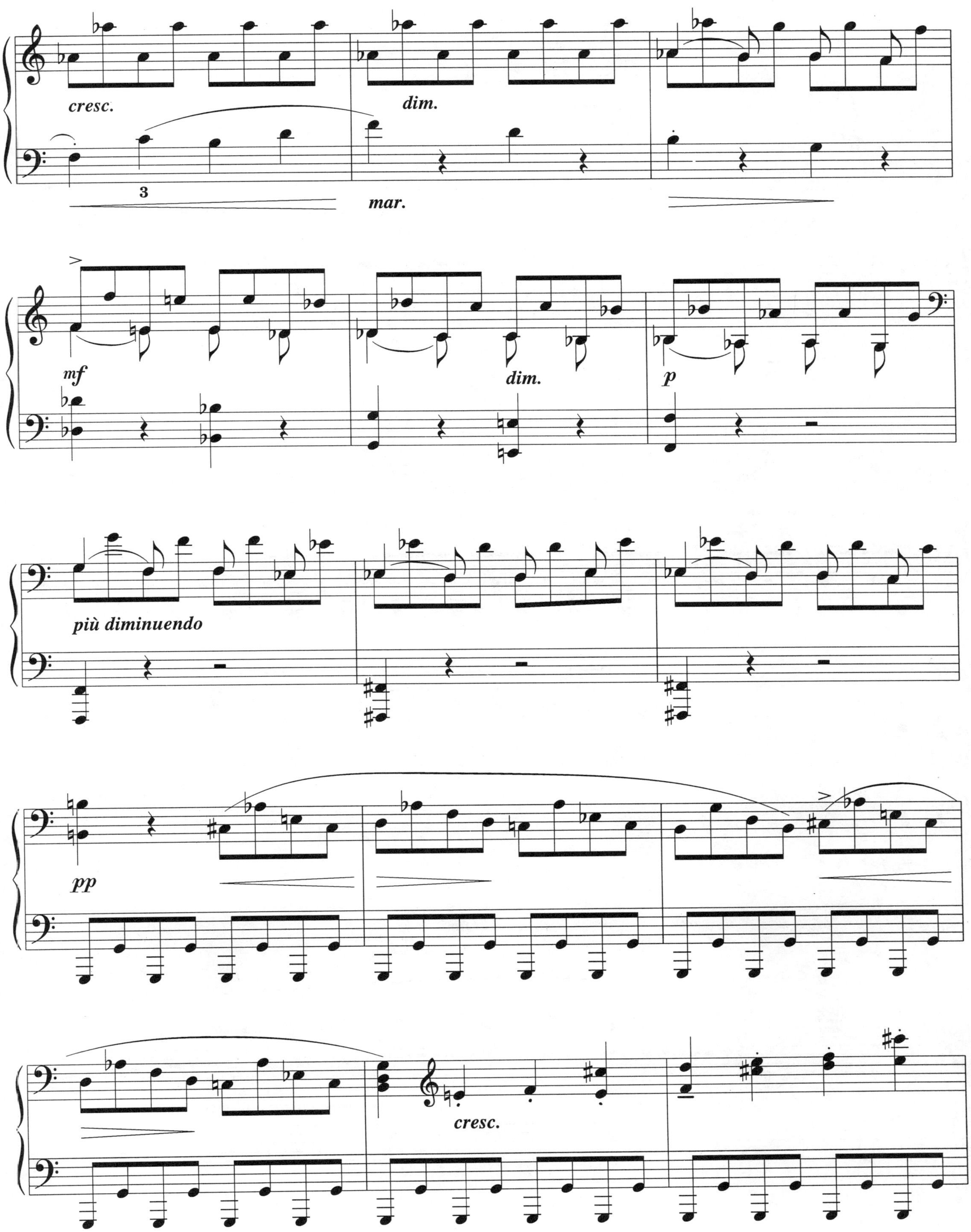
cresc.
dim.
3
mar.
mf
dim.
p
più diminuendo
pp
cresc.

128

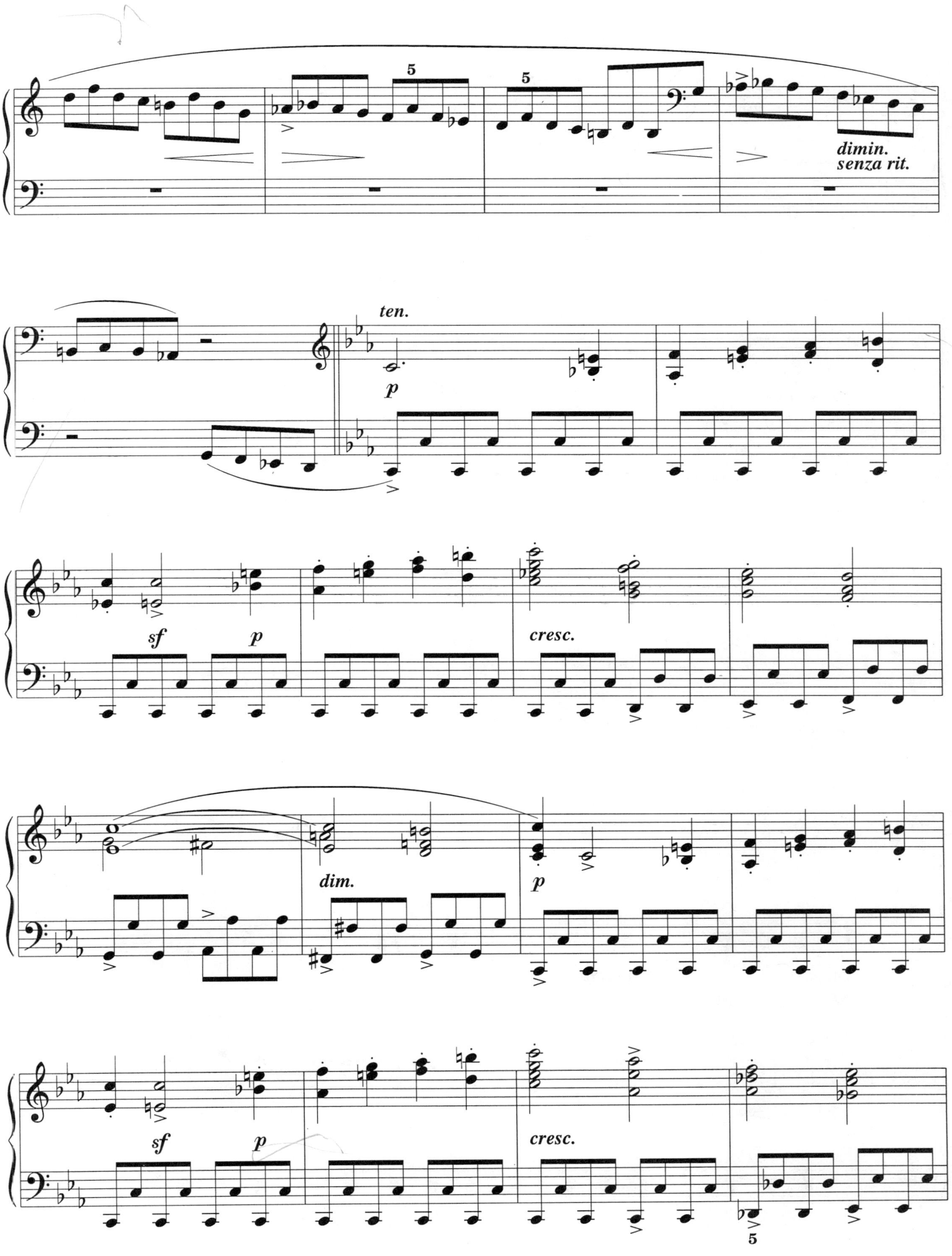
5
5
dimin.
senza rit.
ten.
p
sf
p
cresc.
dim.
p
sf
p
cresc.
5

130

sf
dim.
p
mf
Ped.
p
sf
Ped.
sf
Ped.
p
mf
poco cresc.
decresc.
pp
ben tenuto il basso
a tempo
poco rit.
p legato
Ped.
p
Ped.

132

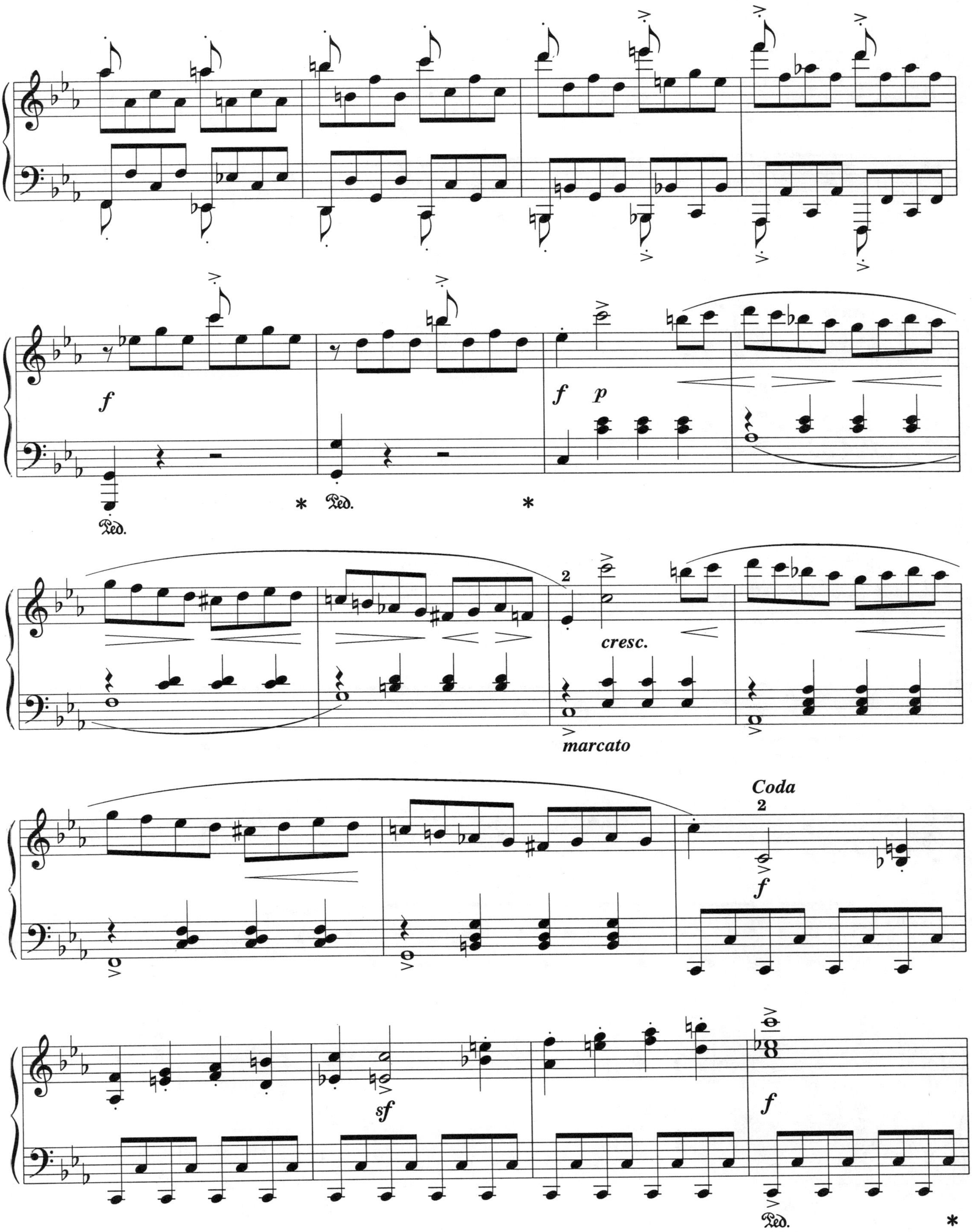

f
Ped.
*
Ped.
*
f p
2
cresc.
marcato
Coda
2
f
sf
f
Ped.
*

piu f
ff
ff
Ped.
*
Grave
p
cresc.
fz
b)
ten.
Allegro molto e con brio
ten.
decresc.
pp
p
sf
p
cresc.
ff
secco
ffz
ffz

Adagio cantabile (♪ = 60)
p sempre legatiss.
p
Ped. *
p
espress.
Ped. *
Ped.
poco meno piano
p
p
Ped. * Ped. *
espress.
mp
p
Ped. *

a piacere
cresc.
dim.
p
mf
dimin.
Ped.
ten.
cresc.
ten.
p
cresc.
Tempo I
ten.
slentando
p
p
p
p
espress.
pp
Ped.

137

138

139

140

141

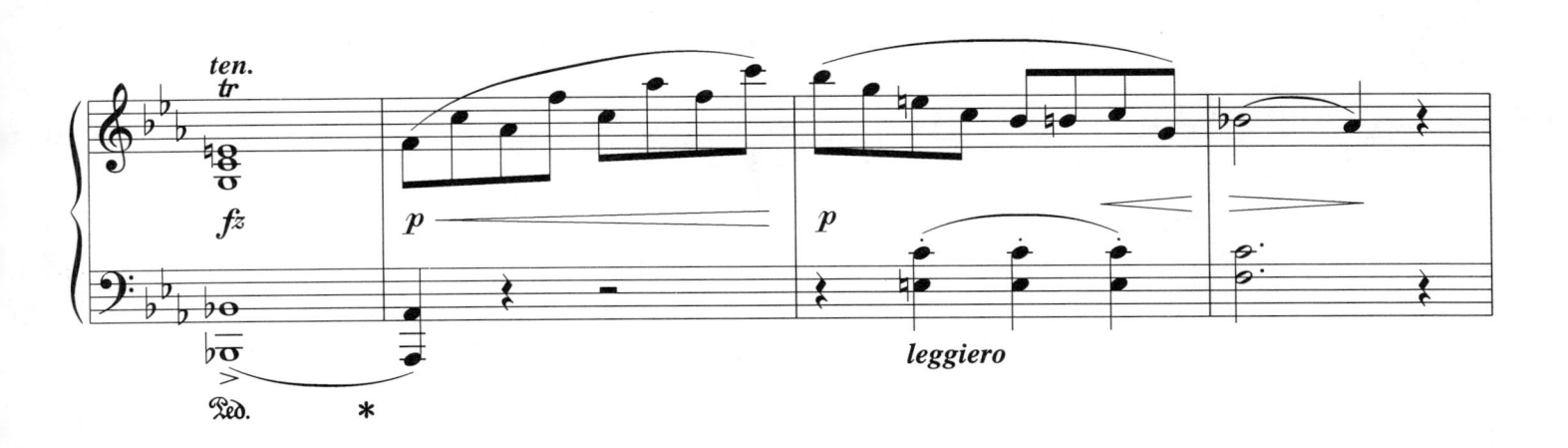

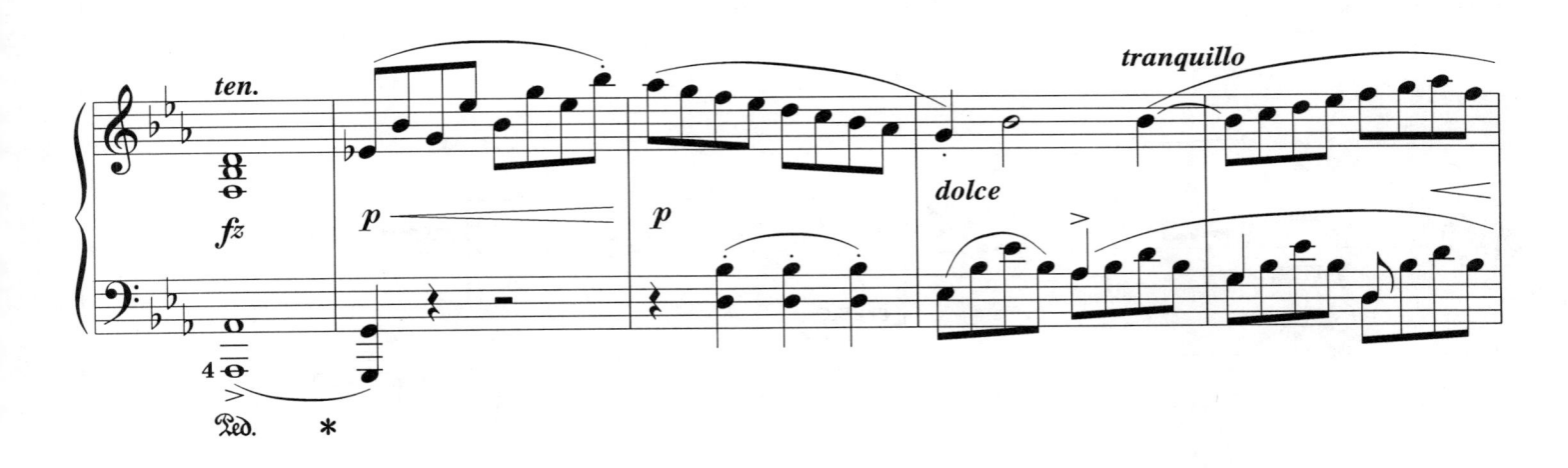

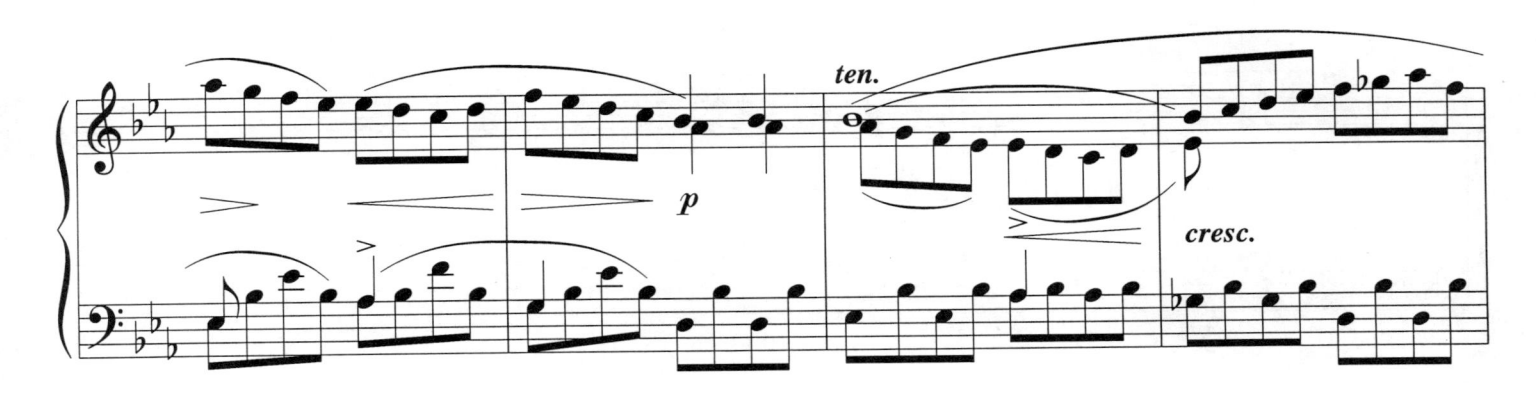

p
sf
p
cresc.
f
dim.
sf
sf
Ped.
*
p
cresc.
1
f
sf
Ped.
*
cresc.
Ped.
*
f
mf
ten.
p
espress.
p
ten.
2
p
poco marcato

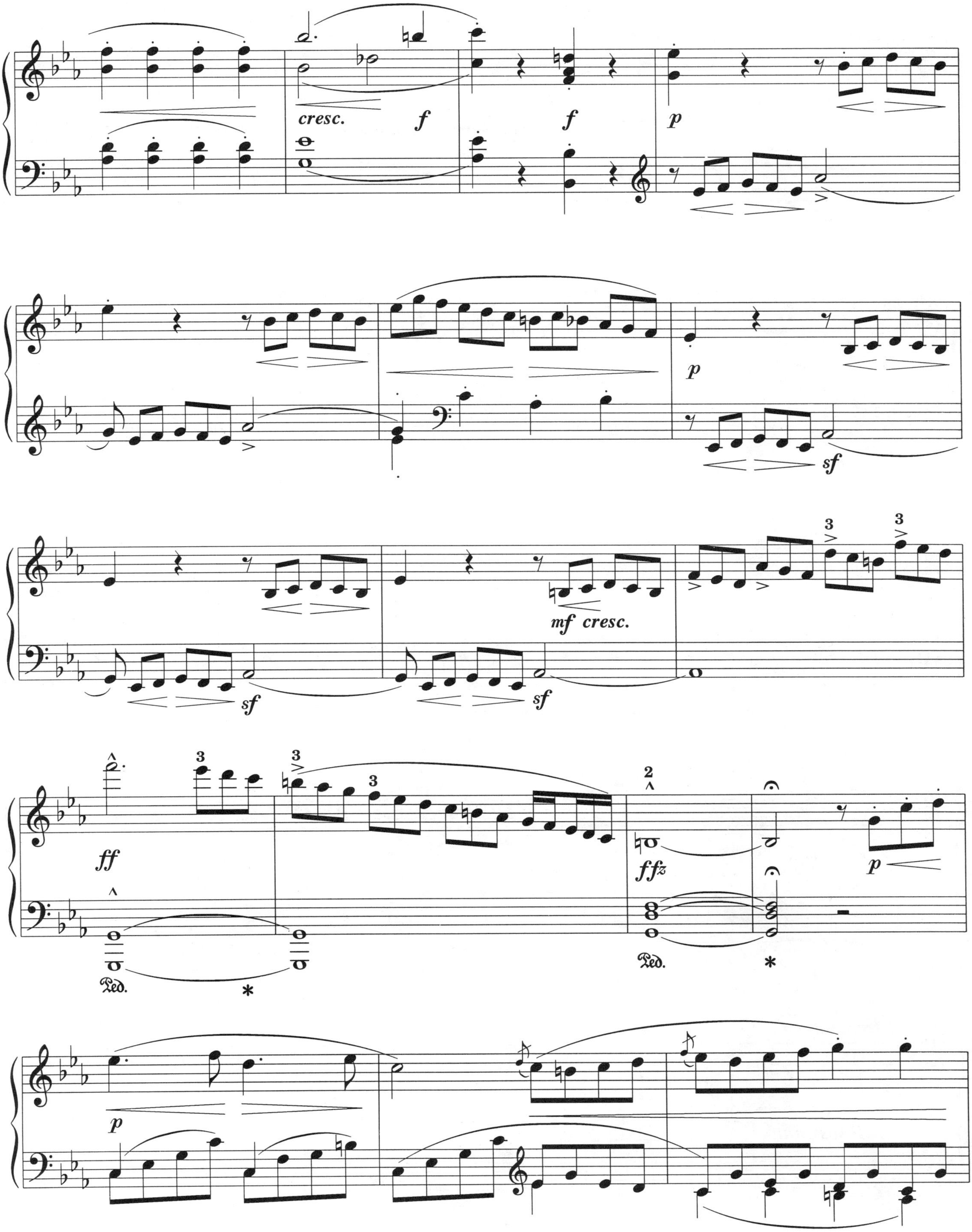
cresc.
f
f
p
p
sf
sf
mf cresc.
sf
ff
Ped.
*
ffz
Ped.
*
p
p

p
mf
mf
p
fz
Ped.
*
fz
p
Ped.
*
cresc.
Ped.
*
mfz
cresc.
tr
f
più f
p
tranquillo
p sostenuto
espress.

mf
marc.
dolce espress.
dim.
p
dolce
espress.
p
cresc.
staccariss.
f
ten.

146

147

148

ten.
p
p
dim.
mf
Con moto
ten.
ten.
ten.
ten.
sostenuto
f
f
calando
cantabile
a tempo
p semplice

150

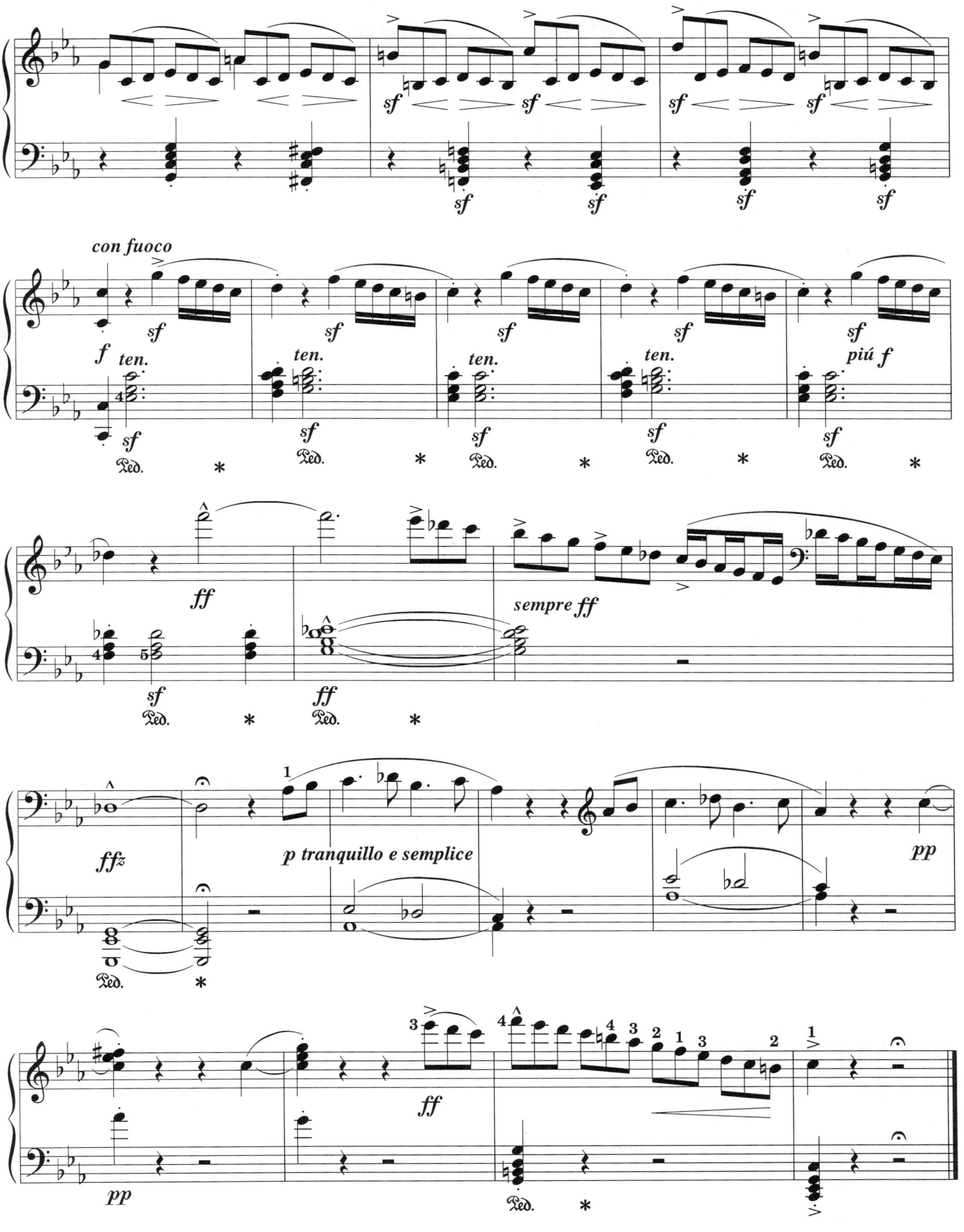

sf
con fuoco
f
ten.
piú f
Ped.
ff
sempre ff
ffz
p tranquillo e semplice
pp